What must I do to be SAVED?

MARCUS GRODI

CHResources
PO Box 8290
Zanesville, OH 43702
740-450-1175
www.chnetwork.org

CHResources is a registered trademark
of the Coming Home Network International, Inc.

Cover design and page layout by Jennifer Bitler
www.doxologydesign.com

INTRODUCTION

A man boldly stepped out of the crowd and asked Jesus, "Teacher, what good deed must I do to have eternal life?" (Mt 19:16). This man was no ordinary man, but a "ruler" (Lk 18:18) of the local synagogue, or "archon" associated with the other religious leaders, Pharisees, and scribes. This meant that he knew his Jewish heritage and tradition.

This "rich young ruler," however, may have heard a sufficient amount of Jesus' discourses and parables concerning the coming of the Kingdom of Heaven to wonder whether the appearance and teachings of this "good teacher" signified some radical change in the order of things—whether there was a new set of requirements for gaining eternal life.

In another instance, a lawyer posed a similar question to Jesus, this time in the form of a test: "Teacher, what shall I do to inherit eternal life?" (Lk 10:25-28).

Jesus responded differently to each of these two seekers. Yet there is a similarity, at least in the eyes of many Christians, for both situations seem to emphasize that salvation is an individualistic matter: "What must I do...?" And the answers that Jesus gave seem to confirm this: in neither case did Jesus mention the necessity of membership in any religious community, the practice of any rituals, the reception of any sacraments, the submission to any leaders, or the adherence to any set of doctrines.

Even in another Gospel account, when the spokesmen for the crowd asked Jesus, "What must we do to be doing the works of God?", His simple answer was, "This is the work of God, that you believe in him whom he has sent" (Jn 6:28-29). Again no mention of community, rituals, sacraments, leaders, or doctrine. What He seemed to emphasize was faith *alone* in Him *alone* for every individual person *alone*.

JOHN 3:16

Most Americans have seen the image of a man, wearing a multicolored wig, standing in the grandstands of a football stadium, holding up a sign that states merely: JN 3:16. Is the man trying to tell the person with license plate number JN316 that his headlights are on? Hardly.

Most modern American Christians, at least, know that when they see this placard—or a similar message on the back of someone's t-shirt or on the side of a barn—it's there because some sincere Bible-believing Christian is trying to help some *individual* come to know Jesus and be saved. They believe that all that is necessary for salvation is for any *individual*—apart from any connection to any institutional church—to turn in a Bible to John 3:16, read the words of "the gospel"—"For God so loved the world that he gave his only Son, that whoever believes in him should not perish but have eternal life"—fall on his knees, pray some form of "sinner's prayer," and, by the work of grace on his heart and mind, accept Jesus as his personal Lord and Savior. At that moment in eternity, the person is then saved. If the person never becomes a member of a church—if he is never baptized, never receives any sacraments, practices any form of liturgy, submits to any leadership, or believes any list of dogma—it doesn't matter eternally: he has accepted Jesus, and is saved.

This idea of individualistic salvation seems to be a growing, if not the majority opinion, at least among modern American Christians. This is true even among those who are members of denominational churches, who practice some set of sacraments or ordinances, participate in some form of liturgical worship, and hold to some credal statements. An underlying suspicion has emerged that, when all is said and done, all that is eternally necessary is faith in Jesus *alone*. Even though the sixteenth-century Reformers assumed that a person needed to belong to some church, hold to some creed, gather for worship, follow their leaders, celebrate at least two sacraments (Baptism and communion), and live by some set of rules, yet, the resultant divided denominational streams differ to such extent that the composite conclusion in this age of tolerance, at least among Evangelicals, is that all that is necessary for salvation is "Jesus and me."

As an Evangelically convicted Presbyterian minister, I admittedly taught and preached that my form of Evangelical Calvinism was the clearest permutation of the Gospel message, yet I never believed or taught that one had to be a Presbyterian, or in fact anything, to be saved, as long as one had surrendered to Jesus Christ. What I did not realize, though, was to what extent this individualistic salvation was a purely modern assumption, and a dangerously truncated gospel.

It was difficult, among compatriot believers and pastors, to identify and agree upon what was missing in this simplistic version of the Gospel that is so pervasive across our country, broadcast on television and radio, preached from innumerable pulpits, and shared on park benches or in the African bush by well-meaning missionaries. I have come to believe, however, that a correct biblical as well as historical understanding of salvation in Jesus Christ involves a whole lot more than an individual's intellectual acceptance and heart-felt prayer of faith in Jesus as Lord and Savior; that salvation involves far more than a mere personal relationship between "Jesus and me."

I realize that most Christian ministers would say they agree, yet in the indifferentism that by necessity exists in our modern Christendom of thousands of separate Christian denominations, I believe that this simplistic "Jesus and me" theology undercuts the core of what it truly means to be a Christian. Most critically, this may leave thousands of sincere, yet misguided souls lost in groundless presumptions—and it may leave those who have led them the "least in the kingdom of heaven" (Mt 5:19).

■ What's Missing From John 3:16

So to begin, let's again consider that simple summary of the Gospel:

> *For God so loved the world that he gave his only Son, that whoever believes in him should not perish but have eternal life.*
>
> *John 3:16*

As concise and important as this verse may be, is it not obvious how inadequately it defines salvation if interpreted apart from its context or without sufficient explanation?

What does this verse preach *alone*? "Whoever believes in him…"—but who is "him"? Take, for example, the limitless opinions of who Jesus was and is: the meaning of His sonship; His relationship with God the Father and the Holy Spirit; the question of His divinity and humanity; or the claim that He was nothing more than a good but terribly deluded teacher. There's not a whole lot of theology in

this one verse. There's no mention of church, sacraments, rituals, holiness, or ministers, or any of the things that most Christians take for granted as somehow "essential" aspects of any particular Christian tradition—the things that set them apart from other Christian traditions.

Assuming the traditional, creedal, and orthodox understandings of Jesus Christ as the divine Son of God, Second Person of the Trinity, Savior, and Lord, this verse then states that anyone who believes in Him "will not perish but have eternal life." And so, does this mean that when a person says some form of believer's prayer, he has arrived—that he will not perish but be saved, guaranteed of heaven? As an Evangelical Presbyterian pastor, I would have answered that if one day that person finds himself standing before the gates of heaven, and God asks why He should let him enter, all the person needs to do is point to Jesus and claim the salvation he has in Him "by grace through faith"—because at some specific moment, possibly fifty or more years before, he had accepted "Jesus as his Lord and Savior."

■ A Biblical Interpretation of Discontinuity

Behind this assumption of individualistic salvation in Jesus Christ is a biblical hermeneutic or interpretation of discontinuity. Essentially, there was an original Plan A for salvation, followed by a new and different Plan B. The original Plan A of salvation, for the Old Testament Jews up until the death and resurrection of Jesus—before Christ freed mankind from sin and death, and before the Holy Spirit and grace was given to open hearts and minds for faith—was through works of the Law. In this Plan A, individuals had to earn their entrance into heaven through works, and it was to these Jews that Jesus targeted His mostly moralistic preaching and parables.

However, since this means of salvation was never truly possible, due to sin and mankind's totally depraved will, God provided a new Plan B in Jesus, which began after His resurrection. Salvation through "works of the law" was replaced by salvation by grace *alone* through faith *alone* in Christ *alone*. The laws and demands of the Old Testament ceased, and the New Testament Church emerged as a new thing, established out of necessity when the Jews rejected the Gospel and Christians were expelled from the synagogues.

Like most modern Christian ministers, I admittedly had a limited knowledge of how the Church of the first few centuries operated or worshipped. Assuming this biblical interpretation of discontinuity, I thus assumed that the Church (or churches) was a new beginning, a "new wineskin"—and not a direct continuity of the Jewish faith and covenantal Family of God. Like most, I presumed that in Jesus Christ, the New Testament was a fulfillment of the Old Testament, which denoted a distinct break between the Testaments: any similarities between Christian worship, ecclesiology, and praxis were purely unnecessary remnants that had not been adequately purged.

THE *ROMAN ROAD*

Assuming this Plan A-Plan B disconnect from the Old Testament, there is an expanded version of the simplistic JN 3:16 gospel presentation that many Christians call  the *Roman Road*. This is a collection of six verses from the book of Romans that are used as an evangelistic technique to guide potential converts through what are commonly called the "four spiritual laws." A tab is placed in the evangelist's Bible at the first verse, and then a note written in the margin leads to the next verse and so on.

This *Roman Road* presentation of the Gospel begins at Romans 3:23—"All have sinned and fall short of the glory of God." The beginning assumption is that the person being evangelized is a sinner and, therefore, separated from God. Then, following the marginal note, the evangelist turns to the second verse, 5:12—"Therefore as sin came into the world through one man and death through sin, and so death spread to all men because all men sinned." Since the person is a sinner, the result then is death, and there is nothing a person can do to prevent this on his own.

Then to the next verse, Romans 6:23—"For the wages of sin is death, but the free gift of God is eternal life in Christ Jesus our Lord." In Jesus Christ, the free gift of eternal life is being offered, and then, Romans 5:8—"But God shows his love for us in that while we were yet sinners Christ died for us."

And finally in Romans 10: 9-10, it's time for the potential convert to respond: "[I]f you confess with your lips that Jesus is Lord and believe in your heart that God raised him from the dead, you will be saved. For man believes with his heart and so is justified, and he confesses with his lips and so is saved."

And so, for example, at an evangelistic crusade when people respond to an altar call and then under the guidance of a counselor confess with their lips that they believe in Jesus and accept Him as their Lord and Savior, they are told that they have received eternal life and are saved. And to cap this off, the evangelist turns to the last verse of the *Roman Road*, 10:13—"For, 'everyone who calls upon the name of the Lord will be saved.'"

Now lest I be misunderstood, this collection of verses from Romans is indeed a faithful kernel of the Gospel message. Every individual person faces the just penalty of his or her sins—death—but God through His mercy, while we were yet sinners, sent His Son to die for our sins and gave us the grace to believe and accept Him as our Lord and Savior.

■ The *Roman Road* Plus

This collection of verses from Romans, though widely used and successful in initiating conversions to Christ, is yet insufficient to address all the questions and issues that arise in a discussion of salvation. This is shown by the fact that further explanations or additional verses are usually added whenever the *Roman Road* is used. Like other pastors, I added my own assortment of "additional steps" along the *Roman Road*. For example, I always added at least four more:

Roman Road 6+1 was Romans 7:6—"While we were living in the flesh, our sinful passions, aroused by the law, were at work in our members to bear fruit for death. But now we are discharged from the law, dead to that which held us captive, so that we serve not under the old written code but in the new life of the Spirit." I added this to reiterate the movement from Plan A to Plan B and, therefore, our freedom in Christ from any form of legalism or "works righteousness."

Next, I added *Roman Road 6+2*, verse 8:1—"There is therefore now no condemnation for those who are in Christ Jesus." Since I didn't feel the original *Roman Road* adequately emphasized "eternal security," I added this to ensure that if a person confessed with his lips and believed in his heart, then he was saved, free from any future condemnation.

But what if the person didn't feel saved? What if he felt like his prayers were just bouncing back off the ceiling? That God wasn't really there, or that God didn't care for the person *individually*?

To address this, I added *Roman Road 6+3*, verse 8:26—"Likewise the Sprit helps us in our weakness; for we do not know how to pray as we ought, but the Spirit himself intercedes for us with sighs too deep for words." In other words, weakened by our sins, we are not even able to commune with

God on our own; we need His help. Even when we feel far from Him, the Spirit is praying secretly for us.

And to confirm the meaning of this, I added *Roman Road* 6+4, verses 8:38-39—"For I am sure that neither death, nor life, nor angels, nor principalities, nor things present, nor things to come, nor powers, nor height, nor depth, nor anything else in all creation, will be able to separate us from the love of God in Christ Jesus our Lord." With this additional verse, I emphasized that once saved, there was nothing that could separate a person from Christ.

This was the basic presentation of the Gospel message that I, as an evangelically-minded Presbyterian pastor, and many others used to train door-to-door evangelists.

■ **Bumps Along the *Roman Road***

I dare say, though, that my Methodist, Pentecostal, Church of Christ, Mennonite, Salvation Army, Lutheran, and Episcopal neighbors used slightly different compilations of verses, emphasizing what they felt was essential to the complete and accurate Gospel message. I assume that we were aware of our differences, and, for the sake of peace in the community, left these potentially volatile differences unaddressed. Yet, I was concerned about what I saw as *bumps* along the *Roman Road*, that I, as an evangelical Presbyterian, couldn't answer.

For example, I realized that in assembling this set of verses from the Apostle Paul's book of Romans, I was not passing along Paul's argument exactly as he had presented it. Instead, the *Roman Road* jumped around from verse to verse out of sequence. The *Road* began with chapter 3 then to 5 and 6 and then back to 5 and then skipping over to 10, and then I added verses back in chapter 7 then 8.

This wasn't necessarily a problem, except that I knew that this *Road* was constructed according to my Evangelical Presbyterian Reformed theology or, dare I say, "tradition," a term I

rarely used. Why was my Evangelical Presbyterian "tradition" more historically authentic or scripturally accurate than those of other Christian "traditions" who also based their faith on the Bible *alone*?

It was a problem because I knew there were verses in Romans that I purposely jumped over and avoided in constructing my *Roman Road* to salvation. One of which was Romans 2:6—"For he will render to every man according to his works." The *Roman Road* conveniently starts after this verse, under the assumption that the Book of Romans is divided by the previously mentioned "biblical interpretation of discontinuity," this verse being an "obvious" reference to life under Plan A.

The problem is, however, that this Plan A-Plan B division is nowhere mentioned in the Book of Romans, let alone anywhere else in the Bible. Rather, it is a *theological interpretation* of the Bible that developed after the Reformation to explain away the apparent "works righteousness" of many of Christ's statements, as well as this and similar statements throughout the other New Testament epistles.

It made me pause to think that faithful, Bible-believing Christians of other traditions took all of Romans seriously, not only parts or sections. So how might one fit 2:6 into the *Roman Road*? What if a person did all the things previously mentioned in the *Roman Road*, yet lived an unholy, disobedient life? What if that person was factious, causing schisms in their Christian community? What would happen when this person died? Doesn't this verse say that every individual person will be held accountable before God for his actions?

Another awkward *bump* along the *Roman Road* was 8:14-17—"For all who are led by the Spirit of God are sons of God. For you did not receive the spirit of slavery to fall back into fear, but you have received the spirit of sonship. When we cry, 'Abba! Father!' it is the Spirit himself bearing witness with our spirit that we are children of God, and if children, then heirs, heirs of God and fellow heirs with Christ, ***provided we suffer with him*** in order that we may also be glorified with him." Here Paul inserted a provision to any presumption of rights to eternal security—the provision of willing suffering for the sake of Christ—which was no part of the Gospel as I understood it.

There were lots of other unexplainable *bumps* along this *Roman Road*, especially if one ventured off the path and looked outside of Romans. For example, here's a verse I particularly could not explain as an Evangelical Presbyterian who taught "once saved—always saved":

> *For it is impossible to restore again to repentance those who have once been enlightened, who have tasted the heavenly gift, and have become partakers of the Holy Spirit, and have tasted the goodness of the word of God and the powers of the age to come, **if they then commit apostasy**, since they crucify the Son of God on their own account and hold him up to contempt.*
>
> *Hebrews 6:4-6*

When I was asked to explain this verse—how someone, who from all outward appearances had accepted Jesus Christ and was saved, could commit apostasy—my knee-jerk response was that they must not have been truly saved: they may have "confessed with their lips that Jesus is Lord," but they must not have truly believed this in their "heart." On the surface this may sound like a valid explanation, but this side step merely emasculates the whole theology of eternal security. If there is always an out-clause, then no one can ever be certain that anyone's prayer of conversion is secure.

And there was another off-the-path *bump* that I avoided— one which I never saw for years!

> *I hope to come to you soon, but I am writing these instructions to you so that, if I am delayed, you may know how one ought to behave in the household of God, which is **the church of the living God, the pillar and bulwark of the truth**.*
>
> *1 Timothy 3:14-15*

Here the Apostle Paul explained—to my bewilderment— that the "pillar and foundation of the truth" was not the Bible, as I assumed, but "the household of God, which is the church of the living God." But *which* church? My Presbyterian denomination, or my local Presbyterian congregation? Or some other denomination or local congregation? Or just the so called "invisible church," as described by John Calvin and the other Reformers? But how can any unseen, unidentifiable association of believers be a "pillar and bulwark" of anything?

But then again, wasn't salvation in Jesus Christ merely an individualistic matter? What difference eternally does it make whether a person is Presbyterian, Methodist, Pentecostal, Lutheran, Anglican, or Catholic? Isn't all that is necessary for salvation faith *alone* by grace *alone* in Christ *alone*?

I avoided this *bump*.

But there were more. In Ephesians 4:1-6, Paul wrote,

*I therefore, a prisoner for the Lord, beg you to lead a life worthy of the calling to which you have been called, with all lowliness and meekness, with patience, forbearing one another in love, eager to maintain **the unity of the Spirit** in the bond of peace. There is **one body** and one Spirit, just as you were called to the one hope that belongs to your call, one Lord, **one faith, one baptism**, one God and Father of us all, who is above all and through all and in all.*

Here Paul was calling all Christian believers to maintain unity, bonded together in the *one body*, which we know from other references means *the Church*; united in *one faith* and *one Baptism*. The problem is that none of the verses along the *Roman Road* mention anything about the necessity of being a member in any one religious community, or adhering to any one set of doctrines, or participating in any rituals or sacraments like Baptism.

To make the *Roman Road* accurate and trustworthy, must we, therefore, add all the verses necessary to cover all these bases? But where and when does one stop, short of including the entire Bible? Which tradition, or which gathering of biblical scholars or theologians, or which individual charismatic leader has the authority to include or exclude, to emphasize or de-emphasize any verse?

In the end, what is eternally necessary for salvation beyond the simple Gospel of John 3:16?

Is there anything at all necessary beyond an individual's relationship by grace *alone* through faith *alone* to Jesus Christ *alone*?

15

GOD DOES NOT CHANGE!

To return to the question posed by those seekers in the Gospel— "What must a person do to have eternal life?"

First, there's an important axiom to consider, that would have been understood and presumed true by those first-century Jewish seekers: God is immutable and does not change. There is a great mystery here—how is it that God plans all things before Creation yet still encourages us to present to Him our needs and deepest desires in prayer—but this is the constant witness of Scripture:

> *For I the Lord do not change; therefore you, O sons of Jacob, are not consumed. From the days of your fathers you have turned aside from my statutes and have not kept them. Return to me, and I will return to you, says the Lord of hosts.*
>
> *Malachi 3:6-7*

> *Every good endowment and every perfect gift is from above, coming down from the Father of lights with whom there is no variation or shadow due to change.*
>
> *James 1:17*

This is indeed an unfathomable mystery, yet most Christians agree that God is omniscient, omnipresent, omnipotent, and, in essence, immutable.

If God, therefore, is immutable, than why wouldn't His criteria for entrance into His eternal presence—for salvation—remain the same over time, even with the coming of Christ?

Maybe, due to His divine wisdom, He did not always reveal His plan in its fullness, releasing it in stages or levels, according to the mystery of His plan of salvation and the receptivity of the people. Or, maybe mankind over the centuries, due to sin and pride, did not hear, understand, or follow His criteria. But is it not possible that the essential criteria for entrance into His eternal presence has always been the same? Certainly the gift of grace in and through the resurrected Christ may have changed how mankind can hear, understand, and fulfill these expectations, but if God is immutable, then why should we not expect His criteria for salvation to always have been constant for Adam and Eve, Abraham, Isaac, Jacob, Joseph, Moses, Joshua, David, Solomon, the Pharisees and scribes, for the Apostles, and for every individual person from the beginning of time down to you and me?

With this as a beginning thesis, how was an individual person "saved" in the Old Testament?

PSALM XXIV:III-VI

We must admit up front that there is no consensus as to what the Jewish people before Christ believed happened after death, or what they always meant in Scripture by the term "salvation." There seems to have been a development, as well as conflicting views concerning the existence of an afterlife.

In Psalm 24:3-6, however, we find a verse similar to John 3:16. The underlying question in this Psalm is "Who shall ascend the hill of the lord? And who shall stand in his holy place?" Or, in other words, "How does one get close to God?" The psalmist seems to give a clear and definitive answer:

> *He who has clean hands and a pure heart,*
> *   who does not lift up his soul to what is false,*
> *   and does not swear deceitfully.*
>
> *He will receive blessing from the Lord,*
> *   and vindication from the God of his salvation.*
>
> *Such is the generation of those who seek him,*
> *   who seek the face of the God of Jacob.*

Imagine, if you will, sitting in the crowd at Ben Hur's chariot race and seeing someone, in a multi-colored robe, hold up a sign with the letters PSALM XXIV:III-VI. Now imagine a Roman centurion rushing home, pulling out a scroll of the Psalms (which he had obtained from his last pillage of a Jewish synagogue), turning to Psalm 24, and, upon being cut to the

quick, having a conversion of heart, reforming his life, cleaning up his language, throwing out his idols, washing his hands, and trying to cleanse the thoughts of his heart. Was this all that any individual during Old Testament times needed to do to obey this Psalm and get right with God?

On the surface, I can imagine myself, as an Evangelical Presbyterian minister, preaching, "Yes—apart from faith in Jesus, of course." This assumption even seems to be reinforced by James 4:8—

> *Draw near to God and he will draw near to you. Clean your hands, you sinners, and purify your hearts, you men of double mind.*

I've come to recognize, however, that this assumption is grossly inaccurate, for by interpreting Psalm 24 apart from its wider context, it truncates what any individual person during Old Testament times would have needed to do to be right with God.

Essentially, what is missing, in both this caricature of Psalm 24:3-6, as well as in John 3:16 *alone* or James 4:8, is what the Jewish authors of all these verses would have assumed their Jewish audiences already understood about the context of these verses. And I believe the Psalmist, as well as the Apostles John and James, would have been shocked to hear how these verses have been used—or should I say abused—when excised from their rightful context.

19

SALVATION IN THE OLD TESTAMENT: THE ASSUMED CONTEXT

So what was the understood context behind Psalm 24? Admittedly, we don't know precisely when this or any of the Psalms were written, but most scholars recognize its constant use by the Jewish people in worship and prayer since the time of King David, if not particularly after the return from exile of Judah to Jerusalem during the liturgical reforms under Ezra the High Priest. Given this, we can conclude that the Psalmist assumed that his hearers were children of Abraham, Isaac, and Jacob—and knew that they had to be.

■ A Child of Abraham

In Genesis 12:1-3, God extended a call and promise to the man from Ur called Abram:

> *Go from your country and your kindred and your father's house to the land that I will show you. And I will make of you a great nation, and I will bless you, and make your name great, so that you will be a blessing. I will bless those who bless you, and him who curses you I will curse; and by you all the families of the earth shall bless themselves.*

This promise was later confirmed by three covenants (Genesis 15, 17, and 22), which were later fulfilled by the Mosaic covenant, the Davidic covenant, and then eventually the New Covenant in Jesus Christ.

To better illustrate the parallels of continuity between the Old and the New Testaments, I'll be summarizing, in panels to the right, what would have been assumed by the Psalmist as, first, the necessary external requirements for any individual who wanted to "ascend the hill of the Lord ... and ... stand in his holy place."

> Children of Abraham

The key point here is that God chose Abram, later given the name Abraham, to be the father of His chosen people, who were to be singularly loyal and holy to the Lord God, to be "his own possession, out of all the peoples that are on the face of the earth" (Deut 7:6). The children of Abraham, Isaac, and Jacob (Israel) were to be witnesses to the rest of the world, but the norm was—by God's mysterious choice—that only those who were children of Abraham could "ascend the hill of the Lord ... and ... stand in his holy place." It was never sufficient to have "clean hands and a pure heart," and knowingly live apart from the chosen people of God. If a person was not a child of the family, there were procedures to become one—to become a child under the kinship bond established by God—but, nevertheless, a person had to become a child of Abraham.

■ A Child of the Covenant

It was not enough, however, to merely be born into the family, for the Old Testament is full of instances where the children of Israel turned from God and as a result reaped God's wrath. Rather, all individual children of Abraham were, also, called to be children of the covenant:

> Children of Abraham
> Covenants

> *I will establish my covenant between me and you and your descendants after you throughout their generations for an everlasting covenant, to be God to you and to your descendants after you.*
>
> *Genesis 17:7*

In these covenants, God established an intimate relationship with His chosen people through Noah, Abraham, Moses, Joshua, and David. These covenants implied a kinship bond, a partnership, between God and His chosen people, which the people were continually called to affirm. These covenants included blessings and curses, and whenever the children of Abraham reaped the wrath of God, it was because they were presuming upon their heritage without being obedient to the covenants. In Psalm 95, for example, we read how, because of their hardness of heart and rebellion against God, He "loathed that generation," and swore in His anger that "they should not enter my rest" (8-11). God, in fulfillment of His side of His covenantal promises, had given them multiple opportunities to repent, but eventually their dirty hands and hard hearts closed the door on God's mercy.

■ The Sign of the Covenant

Merely being a child of Abraham and giving verbal assent to the covenant did not guarantee entrance into God's presence, because there were other criteria. A child of the covenantal family had to accept the signs of the covenants, the most important being circumcision:

> Children of Abraham
> Covenants
> Circumcision

> *This is my covenant, which you shall keep, between me and you and your descendants after you: Every male among you shall be circumcised.*
>
> *Genesis 17:10*

If an individual did not have the sign of circumcision, he couldn't take part in the rituals of the family, like the Passover meal, because he was not a faithful member of the family. However, if an outsider accepted the sign, he could "come near and keep" the Passover, for he now was "as a native of the land. But no uncircumcised person shall eat of it" (Ex. 12:48).

▪ The Law

So, to be able to experience the goodness of God, an individual had to be a circumcised covenantal child of Abraham. This, however, was not enough: there was the Law. Through-

> Children of Abraham
> Covenants
> Circumcision
> The Law

out their sojourning, God had given His people laws, commandments, and ordinances to live by. This began with the Ten Commandments given to Moses on Mount Sinai. Due to the rebellion of the people when they built and worshipped the Golden Calf, God, through His mediator Moses, increased these laws and ordinances, covering nearly every aspect of their lives, as recorded in the Book of Deuteronomy, and then later reiterated by Joshua at Shechem, when he called them to choose which God they would serve (Josh 23:14-16).

Regardless of what stage in the life of Old Testament Israel we consider, therefore, a child of Abraham was to live according to the covenant which meant living in obedience to the Law. This was emphasized in nearly every book of the Old Testament—"Blessed are those whose way is blameless, who walk in the law of the Lord" (Ps 119:1)—and was to be passed down and observed from generation to generation:

> *He established a testimony in Jacob, and appointed a law in Israel, which he commanded our fathers to teach to their children; that the next generation might know them, the children yet unborn, and arise and tell them to their children, so that they should set their hope in God, and not forget the works of God, but keep his commandments...*
>
> *Psalm 78:5-8*

■ Tradition and Scripture

If a circumcised covenantal child of Abraham wanted to be right with God, he, therefore, had to obey the Law, but even this wasn't adequate. Throughout the long history of Israel, besides the laws and ordinances of the Pentateuch, God revealed to Moses, Joshua, the Judges, David, Solomon, and the other leaders and prophets a long tradition of interpretation and implementation of these laws and ordinances. Over time these developed into what became known as the Scriptures, consisting of the Law and the Prophets, and a religious system that regulated the minutiae of people's lives.

> Children of Abraham
> Covenants
> Circumcision
> The Law
> Tradition & Scripture

As Ezekiel was ordered by the messenger of God concerning the new temple arrangements, "… write it down in their sight, so that they may observe and perform all its laws and all its ordinances" (Eze 43:11).

■ Hierarchy

But an individual circumcised covenantal child of Abraham could not merely sit at home with his own scroll of the Law and the Prophets and interpret for himself and his family how they ought to live. Rather, he had to listen to and submit his life to the authoritative hierarchy of leaders and priests that God, through His mediators, had appointed over him:

> Children of Abraham
> Covenants
> Circumcision
> The Law
> Tradition & Scripture
> Hierarchy

> *Moses chose able men out of all Israel, and made them heads over the people, rulers of thousands, of hundreds, of fifties, and of tens. And they judged the people at all times.…*
>
> *Exodus 18:25-26*

> *And Moses wrote this law, and gave it to the priests the sons of Levi, who carried the ark of the covenant of the Lord, and to all the elders of Israel.*
>
> *Deuteronomy 31:9*

■ Ritual

All the above was essential and assumed by the writer of Psalm 24, but still, this wasn't complete, for from the beginning of Creation itself there was liturgical ritual. In fact, the liturgical worship of their Creator God Almighty formed the backdrop for the entire Old Testament, beginning

> Children of Abraham
> Covenants
> Circumcision
> The Law
> Tradition & Scripture
> Hierarchy
> Ritual

with the call to remember the Sabbath day (Ex. 28:8; 31:16) and on through the observance of the various feasts (Leviticus). Few specific details of temple worship are included in the writings of the Old Testament, but in the Psalms we do get a glimpse of their liturgical litanies:

> *O give thanks to the Lord, for he is good,*
> *For his steadfast love endures for ever.*
>
> *O give thanks to the God of gods,*
> *For his steadfast love endures for ever.*
>
> *Psalm 136:1-3*

■ Obedience

So far, we see that, for a person in the Old Testament to be right with God, he had to be a circumcised covenantal child of Abraham, observing the Law and the Prophets, under the authority of Tradition and the hierarchy, and an active participant in the many religious rituals. It was never just God and an individual. Rather they were individuals who were faithful members of God's family, and the bottom line, therefore, was obedience. Hundreds of verses throughout the Old Testament emphasize: "thou shalt keep ... thou shalt obey ... thou shalt walk ... thou shalt not turn away," because there was an understanding that every individual was called to live as a faithful member of the Family of God. If any individual member did not live in obedience, it became the responsibility of the Family of God to carry out the punishments, as stipulated by God through His mediators:

> Children of Abraham
> Covenants
> Circumcision
> The Law
> Tradition & Scripture
> Hierarchy
> Ritual
> Obedience

> *If your brother, the son of your mother, or your son, or your daughter, or the wife of your bosom, or your friend who is as your own soul, entices you secretly, saying, "Let us go and serve other gods,"... you shall not yield to him or listen to him, nor shall your eye pity him, nor shall you spare him, nor shall you conceal him; but you shall kill him; your hand shall be first against him to put him to death, and afterwards the hand of all the people. You shall stone him to death with stones, because he sought to draw you away from the Lord your God...*
>
> *Deuteronomy 13:6-11*

An individual's relationship with God required obedient life within the Family of God.

WAS THIS ENOUGH?

No! Given all of this, it still was not enough, for an individual could be obedient in all these externals—a circumcised covenantal child of Abraham, observing the Law and the Prophets, under the authority of Tradition and the hierarchy, and an active participant in the many religious rituals—yet be lacking an **internal conversion of heart**. This is essentially what the Psalmist was saying in Psalm 24, which emphasized the necessity of both clean hands and a pure heart: if the call for "clean hands" represented the necessary external obedience (pictured in the panels above), the call for a "clean heart" represented the call for an equally necessary internal conversion.

Throughout the Old Testament, God and His spokesmen exhorted the people of God to have an internal conversion of heart. David himself, in possibly his most recited psalm, recognized the need for this as he faced up to his own failures and begged for this conversion:

> CONVERSION OF HEART

> Create in me a clean heart, O God,
>   And put a new and right spirit within me.

> Cast me not away from thy presence,
>   And take not thy holy Spirit from me.

> Restore to me the joy of thy salvation,
>   And uphold me with a willing spirit.

Psalm 51:10-12

■ Hear

The first step in this internal conversion of heart involved *hearing*, which was most notably expressed in

CONVERSION OF HEART
Hear

the great Shema: "Hear, O Israel: the Lord our God is one Lord" (Dt 6:4). This need to *hear* was a constant plea, especially from parents to children throughout every generation: "Hear, my son, your father's instruction, and reject not your mother's teaching" (Prov 1:8). In Hebrew, the same word was used for "to hear" as "to obey," so this conversion of heart was essentially the necessary response to their being faithful members of God's chosen people.

■ Believe

This *hearing* meant more than merely listening to the words; it meant grasping and awakening to their full meaning, and consequent-

CONVERSION OF HEART
Hear
Believe

ly *believing in* and accepting the God who had created them, called and cared for them:

> *Hear me, Judah and inhabitants of Jerusalem! Believe in the Lord your God, and you will be established; believe his prophets, and you will succeed.*
>
> *2 Chronicles 20:20b*

■ Fear of the Lord

This belief was not to stop at a mere mental assent to the existence of God or a person's obligations to Him, but to affect him at the core of his being. The authors of the Old

CONVERSION OF HEART
Hear
Believe
Fear of God

Testament recognized that the beginning of this internal "wisdom" or "knowledge" was the *fear of the Lord* (Ps 111:10; Prov 1:7). The Psalms often expressed that this *fear of the Lord* was necessary for a covenantal child of Abraham to have friendship with God: "The friendship of the Lord is for those who fear him, and he makes known to them his covenant" (Ps 25:14; cf. Ps 103:17-18; Ps 11:5). Therefore, at least in this sense, the *fear of the Lord* is a bit like *grace* in the New Testament, for both are the necessary initial portals through which mankind can know God.

At the core, the *fear of the Lord* meant that a person was to turn away from any false gods and serve only the Lord God in unswerving "sincerity and faithfulness" (Joshua 24:14).

▧ Love of the Lord

This *fear of the Lord* implied a turning towards God in obedience as well as out of fear for His wrath and justice, as expressed by Moses in his second address to the Israelites in Deuteronomy:

CONVERSION OF HEART
Hear
Believe
Fear of God
Love of God

> [F]ear the Lord your God, you and your son and your son's son, by keeping all his statutes and his commandments, which I command you, all the days of your life; and that your days may be prolonged.
>
> *Deuteronomy 6:2*

But quickly after this same speech, Moses reminded the people that their turning to God was also to be done out of love and gratitude:

> Hear, O Israel: The Lord our God is one Lord; and you shall love the Lord your God with all your heart, and with all your soul, and with all your might.
>
> *Deuteronomy 6:4-5*

This *fear and love of God* together implied an *inclining of the heart* toward God (Joshua 24:23), and in that sense a turning of the heart in conversion to God. This was never a one-time turning, but, as witnessed throughout the history of Israel, required a continual turning away from false religions and a turning back toward the God of their fathers, both out of *fear* for the curses that would come from their rebellion, as well as out of faithful *love* for and service to the God who had chosen and saved Israel.

The wisdom here is that in the relationship between an individual member of the people of God and his Creator God, both were necessary: if either of these virtues were absent, the imbalance produced a destructive scrupulosity in either direction. The *love* of God must always have as its wise foundation a *fear* of Him.

■ Love of Neighbor

The child of Abraham, therefore, was to hear, believe, fear, and love God, but this vertical relationship had to be translated into a horizontal relationship with one's neighbor:

CONVERSION OF HEART
Hear
Believe
Fear of God
Love of God
Love of Neighbor

> *You shall not hate your brother in your heart ... but you shall love your neighbor as yourself: I am the Lord.*
> *Leviticus 19:17-18*

This love of neighbor was to be more than what was enumerated in the Law, where boundaries were established on what could or could not be done to a fellow child of Abraham. This love required mercy, forgiveness, even sacrifice, and not just for blood kin, but for anyone within the covenantal community—which was intended to include all the nations of the world, though this was rarely understood during the Old Testament period:

Declare his glory among the nations, his marvelous works among all the peoples ... Say among the nations, "The Lord reigns."

Psalm 96:3,10

■ Holiness

With this call for a vertical relationship with God and a horizontal love for neighbor, the child of Abraham was also called to be holy:

CONVERSION OF HEART
Hear
Believe
Fear of God
Love of God
Love of Neighbor
Holiness

And the Lord said to Moses, "Say to all the congregation of the people of Israel, You shall be holy; for I the Lord your God am holy."

Leviticus 19:1-2

In other words, every individual child of Abraham was to experience what would later be understood as a spiritual journey: through hearing and believing, fearing and loving God, they were to experience a change of heart from hard to contrite, which was to be expressed in love for neighbor and personal holiness, so they could stand before their God without embarrassment.

BUT WAS THIS ENOUGH?

The two panels to the right summarize, therefore, what was assumed necessary, both externally and internally, for a person in the Old Testament to "ascend the hill of the

Children of Abraham
Covenants
Circumcision
The Law
Tradition & Scripture
Hierarchy
Ritual
Obedience

CONVERSION OF HEART
Hear
Believe
Fear of God
Love of God
Love of Neighbor
Holiness

Lord ... and ... stand in his holy place." Yet, was this sufficient to fulfill the expectations of Psalm 24?

No, for there was a problem, called *sin*. All of the children of Abraham had "sinned and gone astray" (Ps 14:3), though the doctrine of original sin would not be recognized and defined for centuries to come. The individual members of the people of God might try to live according to the expectations of their covenantal relationship to God and neighbor, they might try to turn their hearts and minds away from foreign gods, but as repeated throughout the Old Testament, "the people of Israel did what was evil in the sight of the Lord" (Judg 3:12). No matter how hard they tried, in some way every child of Abraham failed to fulfill some, if not all the external and internal demands of their walk as a child in the covenantal Family of God.

SO WHAT WERE THEY TO DO?

God provided the answer, called *atonement*. This deserves, of course, a much fuller description, but suffice it to say that God provided the ceremonies, rituals, and sacrificial means that helped the Old Testament people of God remit their guilt and break from the sin that prevented them from being obedient to the external and internal commitments to God:

> ATONEMENT

> *Then Moses said to Aaron, 'Draw near to the altar, and offer your sin offering and your burnt offering, and make atonement for yourself and for the people.*
>
> *Leviticus 9:7a*

■ Repentance

The liturgical process of atonement involved repentance first, as again expressed in David's famous psalm:

> ATONEMENT
>
> Repentance

> *For I know my transgressions, and my sin is ever before me. Against thee, thee only, have I sinned, and done that which is evil in thy sight, so that thou art justified in thy sentence and blameless in thy judgment.*
>
> *Psalm 51:3-4*

■ **Turning**

This admittance of guilt, however, could not be a mere mental
confession, but required a turning

ATONEMENT
Repentance
Turning

away from all sources of temptation and their "evil ways"
(2 Kgs 17:13).

■ **Sacrifice**

From the very beginning, from
the time of Cain and Abel, repentance and turning was not sufficient
but required a concomitant form of
sacrifice. Because the Israelites failed

ATONEMENT
Repentance
Turning
Sacrifice

to obey the stipulations of Sinai and leave the gods of Egypt
behind them, God through Moses increased the demands and
frequency of their sacrificial rituals:

> But you shall seek the place which the Lord your God will choose
> out of all your tribes to put his name and make his habitation
> there; thither you shall go, and thither you shall bring your burnt
> offerings and your sacrifices, your tithes and the offering that
> you present, your votive offerings, your freewill offerings, and the
> firstlings of your herd and of your flock.
>
> *Deuteronomy 12:5-6*

Throughout the Old Testament, especially in the Psalms
and Prophets, they were warned that their sacrifices were never to consist merely of external acts but were to be expressions
of truly converted hearts:

> I do not reprove you for your sacrifices; your burnt offerings are
> continually before me.

> I will accept no bull from your house, nor he-goat from your
> folds....

> Offer to God a sacrifice of thanksgiving, and pay your vows to the
> Most High;

trouble; I will deliver you, and

Psalm 50:8-15

tire Old Testament, the Psalm-
ment of the external sacrificial
)f heart. Rather, he was declar-
ious practices were empty and
iccompanying internal conver-

ATONEMENT
Repentance
Turning
Sacrifice
Priests

)ns of
f God
)f this
result
olden
borns

·onic and Levitical priesthoods
:s could not make this atone-
ment for themselves or their families—fathers, mothers, and
children in each of their homes killing and sacrificing lambs,
and then eating them every night to atone for the sins of the
day. No, God established the priesthood which shouldered the
responsibility for making atonement for the individual children of Abraham and their families, who were to provide the
sacrificial animals and bring them to Jerusalem on the Day of
Atonement and the other required days of sacrifice.

HOPE?

So, if an individual child of Abraham lived by the above expectations, what was his hope? Even after their exile and consequent return, they continued to believe that God had a hopeful plan for their lives and their nation: "For I know the plans I have for you, says the Lord, plans for welfare and not

for evil, to give you a future and a hope" (Jer 29:11). This hopeful plan would include, among other things:

■ The Restoration of Israel

The Lord Himself like a shepherd would seek out the lost sheep of Israel and restore them as a kingdom on their promised land (Ez 34:11-16):

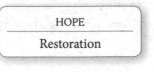

For I will take you from the nations, and gather you from all the countries, and bring you into your own land … you shall dwell in

the land which I gave to your fathers; and you shall be my people, and I will be your God.

Ezekiel 36:24, 28

■ The Messiah

The Lord would "set up over them one shepherd, my servant David, and he will feed them" (Ez 34:23). They, therefore, looked forward to the coming of the Messiah, a Savior, who would reestablish the promised Davidic line and throne, redeeming them from political oppression.

HOPE
Restoration
Messiah

■ The Fulfillment of All God's Covenantal Promises

The coming of this Messiah would bring the fulfillment of all the covenantal promises, which included the promise that Israel would convert the nations of the world:

HOPE
Restoration
Messiah
Fulfillment

And I will vindicate the holiness of my great name, which has been profaned among the nations, and which you have profaned among them; and the nations will know that I am the Lord, says the Lord God, when through you I vindicate my holiness before their eyes.

Ezekiel 36:23

■ New Hearts

All of this restoration would also involve a change within each person:

HOPE
Restoration
Messiah
Fulfillment
New Hearts

I will sprinkle clean water upon you, and you shall be clean from all your uncleannesses, and from all your idols I will cleanse you.

A new heart I will give you, and a new spirit I will put within you; and I will take out of your flesh the heart of stone and give you a heart of flesh.

And I will put my spirit within you, and cause you to walk in my statutes and be careful to observe my ordinances.

Ezekiel 36:25-27

■ Life After Death?

With this hope of restoration for Israel, there was also a growing belief in life with God after death. Throughout the history of Israel, there had developed various opinions as to what awaited the faithful child of Abraham. Generally, they saw life after death as an entrance into *Sheol*:

HOPE
Restoration
Messiah
Fulfillment
New Hearts
Life after Death?

"What man can live and never see death? Who can deliver his soul from the power of Sheol?" (Ps 89:48). By the time of the later prophets and other later Old Testament writings, we begin to see a growing belief in an after-death existence in the presence of God: "Thy dead shall live, their bodies shall rise. O dwellers in the dust, awake and sing for joy" (Is 26:21a).

WHAT ABOUT THE
INDIVIDUALISM OF PSALM 24?

Within this context of faithful membership within the covenantal family of Abraham, the promises of Psalm 24 to a faithful individual make sense. Throughout the Old Testament, the constant call rings out for obedient individualism, especially in the Psalms and Wisdom literature, but always under the assumption of faithful membership within the chosen family of Abraham.

> *Who shall ascend the hill of the Lord ... shall stand in his holy place? He who has clean hands and a pure heart, who does not lift up his soul to what is false, and does not swear deceitfully.*

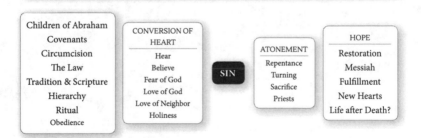

It must be noted that from the beginning, God had been fathering His first-born chosen son, Israel, especially through His long line of covenants in the form of kinship bonds. Nonetheless, the Israelites rarely understood or appreciated this. Even in the few instances where they recognized God as a father, it was too often the fatherhood of one who demanded strict obedience, as that which Jesus described as the expectation of the prodigal son, who understood himself no longer worthy to be treated as a son, but only as a servant (Lk 15:15-17). They generally understood their relationship with God as slaves to a caring, protective, shepherding Creator and Master.

SO WITH JESUS HAVE THESE EXPECTATIONS BEEN SET ASIDE?

As we consider this long list of expectations that were placed upon the shoulders of every individual within the family of Old Testament Judaism, I'm reminded of the "burthen" that impeded the uphill climb of Christian in *Pilgrim's Progress*. A part of me wants to exclaim, "This is precisely what Jesus came to free us from! From slavery under the burden of the Law!"

But as we move our attention from the Old Testament into the New, is there a place where Jesus in fact reduces or eliminates these Old Testament expectations of being a child

of Abraham? Does He, essentially, start from scratch, setting aside all of these external and internal burdensome requirements, making salvation now an individualistic quest based on grace *alone* through faith *alone* in Christ *alone*?

First, it's important to recognize that the hopes of the Old Testament children of Abraham were still alive when Jesus was born, and those who held these hopes still understood the necessity of obedience to the above covenantal requirements. Such was expressed in the prophetic exclamation of the priest Zechariah, who with his wife, Elizabeth, "were both righteous before God, walking in all the commandments and ordinances of the Lord blameless" (Lk 1:6). Through the message of the angel Gabriel and the visit of Mary with his wife, Zechariah knew that at the birth of his own son, John, the time for all of their expectations had arrived:

> *Blessed be the Lord God of Israel, for he has visited and redeemed his people,*
> *and has raised up a horn of salvation for us in the house of his servant David,*
> *as he spoke by the mouth of his holy prophets from of old,*
> *that we should be saved from our enemies, and from the hand of all who hate us;*
> *to perform the mercy promised to our fathers, and to remember his holy covenant, the oath which he swore to our father Abraham,*
> *to grant us that we, being delivered from the hand of our enemies, might serve him without fear, in holiness and righteousness before him all the days of our life.*
> *And you, child, will be called the prophet of the Most High; for you will go before the Lord to prepare his ways, to give knowledge of salvation to his people in the forgiveness of their sins,*
> *through the tender mercy of our God, when the day shall dawn upon us from on high to give light to those who sit in darkness*

and in the shadow of death, to guide our feet into the way of peace.

Luke 1:68-79

This prayer of praise confirms the continuity of the Old Testament expectation right up until the time that Jesus was born. Zechariah was not expecting any radical changes in his life as an individual member of the family of Abraham; rather he was excitedly anticipating the fulfillment of all their hopes.

■ What Did Jesus Preach?

When His time to step into action had come, we are told that, after He accepted baptism at the hands of John and successfully completed His ordeal of temptation in the desert, Jesus came out preaching that "[t]he time is fulfilled, and the kingdom of God is at hand; repent. And believe in the gospel"

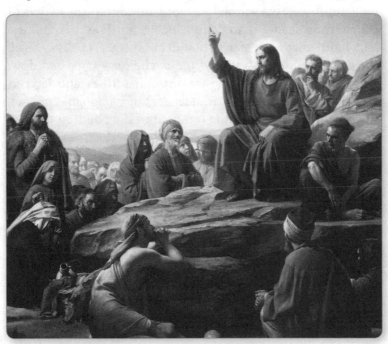

(Mk 1:15). It is significant to recognize that Jesus was speaking to Jews who presumed all of the above expectations of covenantal obedience.

What did Jesus encounter as He traveled around Galilee, preaching, healing, and exorcising demons from the possessed? Though He encountered a religious culture particularly observant of all the external requirements of their faith, Jesus was "grieved at their hardness of heart" (Mk 3:5). Throughout the history of the Jewish people, there had always been a problem of balance, between the externals and internals of the faith (as summarized in the previous panels). Besides aberrant rejection and disobedience of God's laws, there was too often an imbalanced emphasis on the external obedience of covenantal requirements at the expense of an internal conversion of heart.

In time these externally measured demands grew exponentially until, as Jesus warned in a long discourse, the hypocritical pharisaic leaders had bound "heavy burdens, hard to bear, and [laid] them on men's shoulders" (Mt 23:4). As a result, the general understanding of their religion—as passed down from High priest and priests, through scribes and lawyers, Sadducees and Pharisees, from leaders of synagogues down to the common families of the remnant of the children of Abraham—was one of obedience to fulfilling perfectly every "iota" and "dot" of the Law. In response, Jesus accused them of their imbalanced externalism:

> *Woe to you, scribes and Pharisees, hypocrites! for you cleanse the outside of the cup and of the plate, but inside they are full of extortion and rapacity. You blind Pharisees! First cleanse the inside of the cup and of the plate, that the outside also may be clean. Woe to you, scribes and Pharisees, hypocrites! for you are like whitewashed tombs, which outwardly appear beautiful, but within they are full of dead men's bones and all uncleanness. So*

> *you also outwardly appear righteous to men, but within you are*
> *full of hypocrisy and iniquity.*
>
> Mt 23:25-28

What angered Jesus, therefore, was not their burdensome obedience to externals, but that their hardness of heart had overemphasized the importance of externals, turning them into cold, manipulative "works of the Law." And the leaders were making the people do things that they could not, or would not, do themselves.

Jesus, essentially, was preaching to people who had all the basic information they needed to get close to God, "to have eternal life," but through the centuries and through their hardness of heart, this truth had become encrusted and overpowered with half-truths and darkness. And as Jesus and the writers of the New Testament would say, no one—even a circumcised covenantal child of Abraham—could fulfill the requirements that God expected of His children apart from His only begotten Son, Jesus Christ, and the graces He would give.

■ Did Jesus Teach Individualism?

Given the troublesome imbalance Jesus encountered personally within Judaism, did He respond by preaching the simple individualistic message of JN 3:16? He did go forth exhorting them to believe in Him, but always in the context of repentance, obedience, faithfulness and conversion of heart, while at the same time always continuing within the essential aspects of their covenantal life as children of Abraham.

Jesus emphasized that He had been sent "only to the lost sheep of the house of Israel" (Mt 15:24); He never quit attending the temple, or the synagogues when He was away from Jerusalem; His entire earthly life was regulated by the Feasts; He always told those people He healed to present themselves to the priests, to follow the ritual requirements; and He told His followers, "The scribes and the Pharisees sit on Moses' seat, so practice and observe whatever they tell you, but not what they do; for they preach, but do not practice" (Mt 23:2-3).

Most significantly, though, Jesus made an important reaffirmation during His Sermon on the Mount. He said that He had not come "to abolish the law and the prophets" but "to fulfill them" (Mt 5:17). In fact, He said:

> *For truly, I say to you, till heaven and earth pass away, not an iota, not a dot, will pass from the law until all is accomplished.*
>
> *Matthew 5:18*

Jesus had not come to eliminate but to fulfill all the expectations of their covenantal lives as children of Abraham, as delivered in "the law and the prophets." And since "heaven and earth" are still very much here, this fulfillment has not yet been accomplished.

Jesus also said that anyone who "relaxes one of the least of these commandments and teaches men so"—in other words, who teaches that Christians no longer need to follow the teachings of "the law and the prophets"—"shall be called least in the kingdom of heaven" (Mt 5:19)—in other words, they are not in line with the teachings of Christ.

The reason Jesus came, as alluded to in John 3:16, was not to free people from a supposed religion of "works righteousness" so they could practice a religion of individualistic faith *alone*; rather, after centuries of cyclical rebellion, disobedience, exile, and renewal, culminating in a time of compounded traditions, political oppression, confusion, and hardness of heart, Jesus came to bring redemption and new life, light and truth, for He was the "true light that enlightens every man" (Jn 1:9).

■ The Son of Man Must Be Lifted Up

Maybe Jesus' most telling statement was in the verses immediately preceding John 3:16, describing His encounter with a Pharisee named Nicodemus. Like the seeker mentioned in the beginning, Nicodemus also was a "ruler of the Jews," and therefore, a man of influence, sufficiently aware of the requirements of being a child of Abraham.

John states that Nicodemus "came to Jesus by night," which, besides the obvious, implied that he came to Jesus lost in the darkness and confusion of his Age. Like the "rich young ruler," he recognized, by the signs that Jesus performed, that this man from Galilee was no normal itinerant preacher but a teacher blessed by God.

This entire Gospel account warrants a thorough study, but after Jesus saw that Nicodemus was not going to *see* or *hear* what He was saying concerning the need to be reborn through the waters of Baptism (Jn 3:1-13), Jesus drew Nicodemus back to a key event in the corporate memory of Israel, to something he might understand:

> *And as Moses lifted up the serpent in the wilderness, so must the Son of man be lifted up, that whoever believes in him may have eternal life.*
> John 3:14-15

When this event occurred centuries before in the life of Israel, as recorded in Numbers 21, Moses was not telling the people to abandon all the external aspects, the laws and ordinances of their lives as children of Abraham but to, instead, this one thing—look to the serpent on a stick. Rather, as faithful children of the covenant, they were to turn their attention away from their suffering, their confusion, their ungrateful rebellion, and focus on the image of the serpent which God had given them as a sign of His power and mercy. Looking on the serpent was an act of their trust and obedience, their fear and love of God, which then was to put into focus everything else in their lives.

This, then, was the immediate context for Jn 3:16—"For God so loved the world that he gave his only Son, that whoever believes in him should not perish but have eternal life"— which was followed up by more statements of clarification:

> *For God sent the Son into the world, not to condemn the world, but that the world might be saved through him. He who believes in him is not condemned; he who does not believe is condemned already, because he has not believed in the name of the only Son of God.*

> *And this is the judgment, that the light has come into the world, and men loved darkness rather than light, because their deeds were evil. For every one who does evil hates the light, and does not come to the light, lest his deeds should be exposed. But he who does what is true comes to the light, that it may be clearly seen that his deeds have been wrought in God.*

> *John 3:17-21*

In this context, therefore, Jesus was calling Nicodemus and all lost children of Abraham to "turn from their wicked ways," from their confusion, and look upon Jesus, to put their trust in Him and believe in Him. It did not constitute abandoning their membership in the covenantal Family of God for some form of individualism, but rather it brought focus, bearing, and clarification to their lives in the family.

An incident in Luke 13 likewise illustrates that Jesus was not telling His followers that membership in the covenantal Family of God was insignificant, but rather that in Him they were to achieve a balance of external obedience and internal conversion of heart:

*Now he was teaching in one of the synagogues on the sabbath.…
But the ruler of the synagogue, indignant because Jesus had
healed on the sabbath, said to the people, "There are six days on
which work ought to be done; come on those days and be healed,
and not on the sabbath day."*

*Then the Lord answered him, "You hypocrites! Does not each of
you on the sabbath untie his ox or his ass from the manger, and
lead it away to water it? And ought not this woman, a daughter
of Abraham whom Satan bound for eighteen years, be loosed
from this bond on the sabbath day?"*

*As he said this, all his adversaries were put to shame; and all the
people rejoiced at all the glorious things that were done by him.*

Luke 13:10-17

Here Jesus was faithfully following the rituals of being a
son of Abraham, and did not tell His audience to do otherwise,
whereas the ruler of the synagogue, so blinded by his hardness
of heart, was caught up in hyper, scrupulous externalism.

Throughout His earthly ministry, Jesus was calling the children of Abraham to augment their obedience to the external
ordinances of their faith with a complete conversion of heart,
through a conversion to Him as their long-awaited Messiah.
Jesus was then lifted up so that in the midst of their confusion
and darkness, they might turn and put their faith in Him.

SALVATION IN THE NEW TESTAMENT

The bottom line is that nowhere does Jesus tell His followers that there was to be a radical shift from salvation as a faithful individual in the Family of God to an isolated individual whose relationship with Him was based on grace *alone* through faith *alone*. Rather we see throughout His ministry and teaching, and on into the early life of the Church, a continuity between the Old Testament "law and the prophets" and the New Testament following of Jesus.

■ The New Family of God

The difference is that every single aspect of what was summarized

> The new Family of God

above was touched, fulfilled, and renewed in Jesus—He was bringing them new life in the new Family of God.

Jesus told His audience that He was "sent only to the lost sheep of the house of Israel" (Mt 15:24), but it had always been God's desire that Israel, His chosen first-born, was to be a witness to the nations. Jesus sent His hand-chosen Apostles out with the clear instruction to go "to the lost sheep of the house of Israel. And preach as you go, saying, 'The kingdom of heaven is at hand'" (Mt 10:6-7). The coming of Jesus was the fulfillment of the long-awaited promises to David, but, as was proclaimed by the prophets of the Old Testament as well as in His own teachings, this was going to be a new Israel, an expanded Israel, that would include all nations, a salvation which God had "prepared in the presence of all peoples, a light for revelation to the Gentiles, and for glory to thy people Israel" (Lk 2:30-31).

And this new Israel was fulfilled when Jesus established His Church in His twelve hand-chosen Apostles, when he said, "I will build my church, and the powers of death shall not prevail against it" (Mt 16:18).

> The Church

The Apostle Paul identified this Church as "his body, the fullness of him who fills all in all" (Eph 1:22-23) and as "the household of God, which is the church of the living God, the pillar and bulwark of the truth" (1 Tim 3:15).

The new Israel is the Church, the continuity of the covenantal children of Abraham.

■ The New Covenant

Through the Prophets, the Old Testament children of Abraham were promised that one day God would make a new covenant with them:

> The Church
> The New Covenant

> [T]he days are coming, says the Lord, when I will make a new covenant with the house of Israel and the house of Judah.
>
> *Jeremiah 31:31*

And both Luke and Paul wrote that this new covenant has now been established in the cup of the blood of Christ:

> *And likewise the cup after supper, saying, "This cup which is poured out for you is the new covenant in my blood."*
>
> *Luke 22:20*

> *In the same way also the cup, after supper, saying, "This cup is the new covenant in my blood. Do this, as often as you drink it, in remembrance of me."*
>
> *1 Corinthians 11:25*

Long before the New Covenant or Testament became the title for a canonical collection of documents, it specifically designated the Body and Blood of Christ as the fulfillment of all the Old Testament covenantal promises. This new covenant did not abrogate the old covenant at Sinai but prolonged and renewed it. The blood of the covenant is Christ's, given for the sake of the world.

The author of the Book of Hebrews described this transition clearly:

> *But as it is, Christ has obtained a ministry which is as much more excellent than the old as the covenant he mediates is better, since it is enacted on better promises. For if that first covenant had been faultless, there would have been no occasion for a second. For he finds fault with them when he says: "The days will come, says the Lord, when I will establish a new covenant with the house of Israel and with the house of Judah; not like the covenant that I made with their fathers on the day when I took them by the hand to lead them out of the land of Egypt; for they did not continue in my covenant, and so I paid no heed to them, says the Lord. This is the covenant that I will make with the house of Israel after those days, says the Lord: I will put my laws into their minds, and write them on their hearts, and I will be their God, and they shall be my people. And they shall not teach every one his fellow or every one his brother, saying, 'Know the Lord,' for all shall know me, from the least of them to the greatest. For I will be merciful toward their iniquities, and I will remember their sins no more."*
>
> *In speaking of a new covenant he treats the first as obsolete. And what is becoming obsolete and growing old is ready to vanish away.*
>
> Hebrews 8:6-13

> *Therefore he is the mediator of a new covenant, so that those who are called may receive the promised eternal inheritance, since a*

death has occurred which redeems them from the transgressions under the first covenant.

Hebrews 9:15

■ A New Covenantal Sign

As with all the Old Testament covenants, there is a new covenantal sign, Baptism, replacing that of circumcision:

> The Church
> New Covenant
> Baptism

*In him also you were circumcised with a circumcision made without hands, by putting off the body of flesh in the circumcision of Christ; and you were buried with him in **baptism**, in which you were also raised with him through faith in the working of God, who raised him from the dead.*

Colossians 2:11-12

*... God's patience waited in the days of Noah, during the building of the ark, in which a few, that is, eight persons, were saved through water. **Baptism**, which corresponds to this, now saves you, not as a removal of dirt from the body but as an appeal to God for a clear conscience, through the resurrection of Jesus Christ, who has gone into heaven and is at the right hand of God, with angels, authorities, and powers subject to him.*

1 Peter 3:20-22

*Do you not know that all of us who have been baptized into Christ Jesus were **baptized** into his death? We were buried therefore with him by **baptism** into death, so that as Christ was raised from the dead by the glory of the Father, we too might walk in newness of life. For if we have been united with him in a death like his, we shall certainly be united with him in a resurrection like his.*

Romans 6:3-5

The Early Church writers affirmed that in Christ the sacrifices of the Old Testament covenants ceased and that Baptism was spiritual circumcision:

> *And we, who have approached God through Him, have received not carnal, but spiritual circumcision, which Enoch and those like him observed. And we have received it through baptism, since we were sinners, by God's mercy; and all men may equally obtain it.*
>
> *Justin Martyr, Second Apology, Ch. 43*

It is significant to note that after Peter's first sermon, when his hearers asked what they should do in response, Peter did not say, "Each of you must accept Jesus as your personal Lord and Savior." Rather, he continued the message of John the Baptist and Jesus, confirming the signal importance of Baptism:

> *Repent, and be baptized every one of you in the name of Jesus Christ for the forgiveness of your sins, and you shall receive the gift of the Holy Spirit. For the promise is to you and to your children and to all that are far off, every one whom the Lord our God calls to him.*
>
> *Acts 2:37-39*

And in the final Great Commission that Christ gave His Apostles, He specifically emphasized the importance of Baptism:

> *Go therefore and make disciples of all nations, baptizing them in the name of the Father and of the Son and of the Holy Spirit, teaching them to observe all that I have commanded you; and lo, I am with you always, to the close of the age.*
>
> *Matthew 28:19-20*

Baptism, particularly, emphasizes the communal aspect of our salvation, for we cannot baptize ourselves. Rather, through the hands of the Church we receive Baptism as individuals and, thereby, become members of the Body of Christ, and this is not limited to individual adult believers, but open to every member of the family, regardless of age or intellect (cf. Acts 16:15, 33).

■ A New Commandment

In this new covenantal family we also see that the old Law has been subsumed in a new commandment. Early on, when Jesus was confronted

> The Church
> New Covenant
> Baptism
> New Commandment

by that lawyer seeking answers on how to attain eternal life, Jesus confirmed that all of the Law and the Prophets were summarized in the two great commandments: "Love the Lord your God with all your heart, mind, soul, and strength, and your neighbor as yourself" (Lk 10:27-28). But then later with His Apostles, He gave them a new commandment:

> *A new commandment I give to you, that they should love one another; even as I have loved you, that you also love one another. By this all men will know that you are my disciples, if you have love for one another.*
>
> *John 13:34-35*

But what about the "works of the Law" that Paul said were abolished by faith and grace? In an interesting verse often overlooked, Paul made an important confession:

> *But this I admit to you, that according to the Way, which they call a sect, I worship the God of our fathers, believing everything laid down by the law or written in the prophets...*
>
> *Acts 24:14*

The problem with "works of the Law" is the idea that by being obedient we somehow make God obligated to reward us, to bless and save us. This idea emerges from unconverted hearts, from an imbalanced emphasis upon externals, which in reality is little more than a show to God and to others. This is comparable to children who obey their parents only to avoid punishment (servile fear) or to reap rewards, rather than out of grateful love.

This is the gist of what Paul meant when he castigated the Galatians for those who hoped to force God's hand through circumcision and other "works of the law":

> We ourselves, who are Jews by birth and not Gentile sinners, yet who know that a man is not justified by works of the law but through faith in Jesus Christ, even we have believed in Christ Jesus, in order to be justified by faith in Christ, and not by works of the law, because by works of the law shall no one be justified.
>
> *Galatians 2:15-16*

This certainly deserves a longer treatment, but simply, Paul's intent was not to free Christians from any obligations to the "Law and the Prophets" (i.e., a biblical interpretation of discontinuity) to a new life of faith *alone* lived in the freedom of the Spirit, for this would lead to the very lawless libertinism he warned about later in Galatians:

> For you were called to freedom, brethren; only do not use your freedom as an opportunity for the flesh, but through love be servants of one another. For the whole law is fulfilled in one word, "You shall love your neighbor as yourself."
>
> *Galatians 5:13-14*

Rather, Paul was not discarding the past and substituting instead free love in the Spirit as the only standard, but insisting that the fulfillment of the "Law and the Prophets" in Christ meant that selfless love, in imitation of Christ, was to be the single motive and measure of life as an individual within the new covenantal Family of God.

■ Tradition and Scripture

In the new covenant established by Christ, the Scriptures of the Old Testament were fulfilled, but not set aside. They were considered inspired (2 Tim 3:16-17), but following the instructions of Christ, His Apostles, guided by the Holy Spirit (Jn 14:15-17, 25-26; 15:26-27; 16:13-14), passed on what He taught them (Mt 28:18), and this apostolic deposit of faith was passed along by word of mouth (Acts 2:42) and in written Gospels and epistles. For over three hundred years, this apostolic deposit of faith was passed along by oral or written tradition (2

> The Church
> New Covenant
> Baptism
> New Commandment
> Tradition & Scripture

Thes 2:15; 1 Cor 11:2; 23f; 15:1-3), along with a growing library of other writings, orthodox as well as heterodox, until toward the end of the 4th century, the Bishops of the Church gathered in councils, at Rome (AD 382) and Carthage (AD 397), to declare which particular writings were to be considered orthodox and licit for reading in Sunday worship. This became what we call the New Testament, and, with the entire canon of the Old Testament, became what we call the Sacred Scriptures.

It is significant to point out that the version of the Old Testament that the New Testament writers and first century Christians used was the Greek Old Testament, called the Septuagint. This can be demonstrated by comparing, in any modern translation, New Testament quotes from the Old Testament. For example, Romans 1:17b is a quote by Paul of Habakkuk 2:4b. The Revised Standard Version presents verses as:

"He who through faith is righteous shall live." Romans 1:17b
"...the righteous shall live by his faith." Habakkuk 2:4b

Why the difference? Was Paul misquoting, or merely summarizing the text from memory, or were the RSV translators manipulating the translation? What is significant is that the RSV Old Testament, like most modern translations, is based upon the Hebrew version of the Old Testament, not the Greek Septuagint. However, if one compares the Greek Septuagint version of Habakkuk 2:4b with the Greek New Testament version of Romans 1:17b, one finds that they are almost identical, and

> ο δὲ δίκαιος εκ πίστεως ζήσεται
> *Romans 1:17*
>
> ο δὲ δίκαιος εκ πίστεως μού ζήσεται
> *Habakkuk 2:4b*

read literally, "but the righteous by (their) faith shall live."

What is significant about this is that the Septuagint Greek Version contained all the books of the Old Testament, as confirmed by the 4th century councils and promulgated in all copies of the Scriptures, until some books were removed in the 16th century by Reformers who diverted their emphasis away from the Septuagint to the Hebrew version.

This collection of canonical writings, however, was never intended to be a sole written authority of faith, but with the Sacred Tradition was the rule of faith for the new covenantal Family of God, the Body of Christ, the Church. Most of the early heresies were driven by individuals who promulgated creative ideas based on private interpretations of the Bible *alone* over the received Tradition of the Body of Christ. For example, the doctrines of the Trinity and the Divinity of Christ do not find their source in the Scriptures *alone* but in the continual voice of Tradition and the apostolic deposit of faith, passed down from the beginning, preserved, protected, and promulgated by the Church.

▪ A New Hierarchy

In His choosing, appointing, and anointing of the twelve Apostles, Jesus was fulfilling the patriarchal structure of Israel and the twelve tribes of Jacob (Israel) by establishing a new hierarchy, a new Israel.

> The Church
> New Covenant
> Baptism
> New Commandment
> Tradition & Scripture
> Hierarchy

When Paul and Barnabas wanted to make sure they had the authority to preach, they were sent to Jerusalem to receive confirmation from the Apostles and the Elders (Gal 1:18-2:10). Then Paul in turn appointed his assistants and successors (Tit 1:5; 1 Tim 1:3f), who were to "equip the saints for the work of the ministry" (Eph 4:11-12), and told them to do likewise (2 Tim 2:2). All future leaders and pastors were to be "sent" by the authority of the Church (Rom 10:14-15), and any major decisions that affected the lives of all the believers in their local gatherings were to be decided by meetings called by the leadership (Apostles and Elders) gathered in councils (Acts 15).

The decision of this first council of Jerusalem, as described in Acts 15, is significant in that it established from the beginning that the hierarchy of the Church had the authority to interpret and modify the demands of the Old Testament Law as recorded in Scripture. In this case, the Jerusalem apostolic leadership declared that the law of circumcision was set aside for all future converts to the Church, and that, led by the Holy Spirit, they required "no greater burden than these necessary things: that you abstain from what has been sacrificed to idols and from blood and from what is strangled and from unchastity. If you keep yourselves from these, you will do well" (Acts 15:28-29). In this, we see that from the beginning the Church was not to be a strict religion of the Bible *alone*—which was the position of those Judaizers who were demanding strict observance of the Old Testament regulations—but rather it was to be a Church guided by the Holy Spirit expressed through what has been called the "three-legged stool" of authority: Sacred Tradition, Sacred Scripture, and the authoritative leadership (magisterium) of the Church in union with Peter.

And this last part, "in union with Peter," is important, for it, too, is a continuity with the Old Covenant. When Jesus promised that He would establish His Church, the New Jerusalem, He did so with a specific reference to the Apostle Simon:

> *And Jesus answered him, "Blessed are you, Simon Bar-Jona! For flesh and blood has not revealed this to you, but my Father who is in heaven. And I tell you, you are Peter [Cepha in Aramaic], and on this rock [Cepha in Aramaic] I will build my church, and the powers of death shall not prevail against it. I will give you the keys of the kingdom of heaven, and whatever you bind on earth shall be bound in heaven, and whatever you loose on earth shall be loosed in heaven."*

> Matthew 16:17-19

Here Jesus is making a direct reference to the prophesy of Isaiah when the Davidic king will delegate his own authority, and the "key" that represents this authority, to his next in command:

> *In that day I will call my servant Eli'akim the son of Hilki'ah, and I will clothe him with your robe, and will bind your girdle on him, and will commit your authority to his hand; and he shall be a father to the inhabitants of Jerusalem and to the house of Judah. And I will place on his shoulder the key of the house of David; he shall open, and none shall shut; and he shall shut, and none shall open.*

> Isaiah 22:20-22

The establishment of Simon Peter as the head of the Apostles is the fulfillment of the continuity of the hierarchy of Israel, and this is witnessed throughout the New Testament whenever Peter is mentioned first in the order of Apostles and up front as leader (Acts 1:15; 2:14; 15:7f). It was also affirmed when Jesus commanded Peter to accept the shepherding role over the brethren (Lk 22:32; Jn 21:15-17). This is particularly illustrated by the Jerusalem Council mentioned earlier, for the decision reflected the divine revelation already given to Peter (Acts 10 and 11). Indeed, the two most basic issues with regard to our Lord Jesus were His identity and the scope of His earthly mission, and both of these were settled by divine revelation to Simon Peter (Matthew 16:16-17 and Acts 10:9-16).

This authority of the hierarchy over the members of the growing yet dispersed first-century Church is illustrated throughout the New Testament, as well as in the writings of the Early Church. For example, the Apostle Paul, a prisoner in Rome, wrote a letter to Titus, his "true child in a common faith," who was serving as bishop in Crete—a long thousand-mile journey away by sea—with an authority that squelches any idea of individualistic Christianity:

> *Remind them to be submissive to rulers and authorities, to be obedient, to be ready for any honest work, to speak evil of no one, to avoid quarreling, to be gentle, and to show perfect courtesy toward all men.*
>
> *Titus 3:1-2*

■ Liturgical Worship

There is also a direct continuity between the Old Covenant and New Covenant worship. The significant difference is that the complex temple sacrificial rituals were replaced by the sacramental communion of the Body and Blood of Christ, which is outlined in the first gathering of converts:

> The Church
> New Covenant
> Baptism
> New Commandment
> Tradition & Scripture
> Hierarchy
> Worship

> *And they devoted themselves to the apostles' teaching and fellowship, to the breaking of bread and the prayers.*
>
> *Acts 2:42*

In a microcosm, we find here the structure of liturgy as passed down and witnessed in the earliest writings of the Church. Jesus gave clear instructions to His Apostles in the upper room to do this continually "in remembrance of me"

(1 Cor 11:24), and we see this carried out, for example, in the writings of Justin Martyr (ca. AD 150), which is given here in full length, because it shows the continuity of the liturgical worship of the early Church with that celebrated in most liturgical churches today:

> But we, after we have thus washed him who has been convinced and has assented to our teaching, bring him to the place where those who are called brethren are assembled, in order that we may offer hearty prayers in common for ourselves and for the baptized [illuminated] person, and for all others in every place, that we may be counted worthy, now that we have learned the truth, by our works also to be found good citizens and keepers of the commandments, so that we may be saved with an everlasting salvation.
>
> Having ended the prayers, we salute one another with a kiss. There is then brought to the president of the brethren bread and a cup of wine mixed with water; and he taking them, gives praise and glory to the Father of the universe, through the name of the Son and of the Holy Ghost, and offers thanks at considerable length for our being counted worthy to receive these things at His hands.
>
> And when he has concluded the prayers and thanksgivings, all the people present express their assent by saying Amen. This word Amen answers in the Hebrew language to "genoito" [so be it]. And when the president has given thanks, and all the people have expressed their assent, those who are called by us deacons give to each of those present to partake of the bread and wine mixed with water over which the thanksgiving was pronounced, and to those who are absent they carry away a portion.
>
> And this food is called among us Eukaristia [the Eucharist], of which no one is allowed to partake but the man who believes that the things which we teach are true, and who has been washed with the washing that is for the remission of sins, and unto regeneration, and who is so living as Christ has enjoined. For not

as common bread and common drink do we receive these; but in like manner as Jesus Christ our Saviour, having been made flesh by the Word of God, had both flesh and blood for our salvation, so likewise have we been taught that the food which is blessed by the prayer of His word, and from which our blood and flesh by transmutation are nourished, is the flesh and blood of that Jesus who was made flesh.

For the apostles, in the memoirs composed by them, which are called Gospels, have thus delivered unto us what was enjoined upon them; that Jesus took bread, and when He had given thanks, said, "This do ye in remembrance of Me, this is My body;" and that, after the same manner, having taken the cup and given thanks, He said, "This is My blood;" and gave it to them alone. Which the wicked devils have imitated in the mysteries of Mithras, commanding the same thing to be done...

And we afterwards continually remind each other of these things. And the wealthy among us help the needy; and we always keep together; and for all things wherewith we are supplied, we bless the Maker of all through His Son Jesus Christ, and through the Holy Ghost.

And on the day called Sunday, all who live in cities or in the country gather together to one place, and the memoirs of the apostles or the writings of the prophets are read, as long as time permits; then, when the reader has ceased, the president verbally instructs, and exhorts to the imitation of these good things.

Then we all rise together and pray, and, as we before said, when our prayer is ended, bread and wine and water are brought, and the president in like manner offers prayers and thanksgivings, according to his ability, and the people assent, saying Amen; and there is a distribution to each, and a participation of that over which thanks have been given, and to those who are absent a portion is sent by the deacons.

And they who are well to do, and willing, give what each thinks fit; and what is collected is deposited with the president, who succours the orphans and widows and those who, through sickness or any other cause, are in want, and those who are in bonds and the strangers sojourning among us, and in a word takes care of all who are in need.

But Sunday is the day on which we all hold our common assembly, because it is the first day on which God, having wrought a change in the darkness and matter, made the world; and Jesus Christ our Saviour on the same day rose from the dead. For He was crucified on the day before that of Saturn (Saturday); and on the day after that of Saturn, which is the day of the Sun, having appeared to His apostles and disciples. He taught them these things, which we have submitted to you also for your consideration.

Justin Martyr, First Apology, Ch. LXV-LXVII

■ Obedience

And in this new covenantal family there is a clear call to obedience. Most of the writings of the New Testament consist of instructions on how baptized members of the Body, the Church, are to live together in holiness (cf. Eph 4-6), and if members refuse, they are to be disciplined by the Church.

For example, Paul demonstrates this when he gave instructions on handling an occasion of immorality in the Corinthian Church (1 Cor 5:1-5), acting upon his own apostolic authoritative leadership, but following in obedience the clear instructions of Jesus Himself:

> The Church
> New Covenant
> Baptism
> New Commandment
> Tradition & Scripture
> Hierarchy
> Worship
> Obedience

(15) If your brother sins against you, go and tell him his fault, between you and him alone. If he listens to you, you have gained your brother. (16) But if he does not listen, take one or two others along with you, that every word may be confirmed by the evidence of two or three witnesses. (17) If he refuses to listen to them, tell it to the church; and if he refuses to listen even to the church, let him be to you as a Gentile and a tax collector. (18) Truly, I say to you, whatever you bind on earth shall be bound in heaven, and whatever you loose on earth shall be loosed in heaven. (19) Again I say to you, if two of you agree on earth about anything they ask, it will be done for them by my Father in heaven. (20) For where two or three are gathered in my name, there am I in the midst of them.

Matthew 18:15-20

These instructions from Jesus are particularly telling for our topic. If Christianity is primarily a matter of individualism, than why go beyond the one-on-one confrontation of verse 15? Many Christians believe, based on verses 16, 19, and 20, that any gathering of two or three believers constitutes a "church." But if this is true, than why didn't Jesus say that the confrontation should cease with verse 16? Instead, He stressed that when two or more Christian brothers can't agree, the final authority rests in the Church, and specifically the apostolic hierarchy which has the authority to "bind" and "loose" (17-19).

As quoted earlier from Paul's letters, there is a particular way that Christians "ought to behave in the household of God, which is the church of the living God, the pillar and bulwark of the truth" (1 Tim 3:15), and this meant that every individual Christian was "to be submissive to rulers and authorities, to be obedient..." (Tit 3:1-2).

IS THIS ENOUGH?

So far, there is a clear continuity, at least in the first panels of externals, between membership in the Old Covenant Family of God and the New Covenant Church. But just as in the Old Testament, these external requirements of life are not sufficient within the New Covenant Church, although there are many modern Christians who think that membership in a church, Baptism, confirmation, attendance at worship, and obeying the laws of their church are sufficient for pleasing God. When this happens, the externals once again become nothing more than "works of the law."

Clearly the continuing focus of the teaching of Christ, the New Testament writers, and apostolic Tradition is that we also

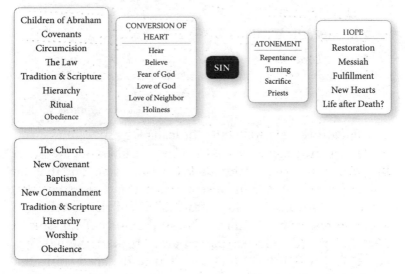

Children of Abraham	CONVERSION OF			HOPE
Covenants	HEART			Restoration
Circumcision	Hear		ATONEMENT	Messiah
The Law	Believe		Repentance	Fulfillment
Tradition & Scripture	Fear of God	SIN	Turning	New Hearts
Hierarchy	Love of God		Sacrifice	Life after Death?
Ritual	Love of Neighbor		Priests	
Obedience	Holiness			

The Church
New Covenant
Baptism
New Commandment
Tradition & Scripture
Hierarchy
Worship
Obedience

need an **internal conversion of heart**. Just as being born into the family of Abraham was not sufficient in the Old Testament (Mt 3:8-9), so being born into the New Covenant Church only gives one a grace-filled opportunity, not a guarantee. Every individual member of the Body must have a conversion of heart, for it is the "pure of heart" who "shall see God" (Mt 5:8).

The process of this conversion is essentially the same as that outlined in the Old Testament:

- It begins with HEARING and UNDERSTANDING (Mt 13:23),
- followed by BELIEVING (Jn 5:24),
- leading to the FEAR OF GOD (2 Cor 7:7),
- and the LOVE OF GOD (Mk 12:29-30),
- which must be shown in LOVE OF NEIGHBOR (1 Jn 2:9),
- and leads to a life of HOLINESS:

CONVERSION OF HEART
Hear
Believe
Fear of God
Love of God
Love of Neighbor
Holiness

May the Lord make you increase and abound in love to one another and to all me... so that he may establish your hearts unblamable in holiness...

1 Thessalonians 3:12-13

Many Christians, following the lead of the sixteenth-century Reformers, believe that in the New Covenant we are saved by grace *alone* through faith *alone* in Christ *alone*, and that the holiness of our lives is inconsequential. This is not, however, what Scripture and Tradition teach, for Paul claimed that (1) every individual baptized member of the Body of Christ is "a new creation; the old has passed away, behold, the new has come" (2 Cor 5:17); (2) that each has been called "to lead a life worthy of the calling to which you have been called, with all lowliness and meekness, with patience, forbearing one another in love, eager to maintain the unity of the Spirit in the bond of peace" (Eph 4:1-3); and (3) that each baptized believer must "appear before the judgment seat of Christ, so that each one may receive good or evil, according to what he has done in the body" (2 Cor 5:10).

Therefore, as Paul exhorted the Corinthian Christians:

Since we have these promises, beloved, let us cleanse ourselves from every defilement of body and spirit, and make holiness perfect in the fear of God.

2 Corinthians 7:1

This was even more emphasized by the author of Hebrews:

Strive for peace with all men, and for the holiness without which no one will see the Lord.

Hebrews 12:14

BUT IS THIS ENOUGH?

A gain, the continuity so far between the Old and New is clear, as fulfilled in Christ. But as affirmed throughout the New Testament, as in the Old Testament, each baptized covenantal child of the New Covenant Family of God is also hindered by *sin* from fulfilling either panel of external or internal obedience. As the Apostle John wrote, "if you say you're without sin then you're a liar. If you say that you have not sinned you don't know him" (1 Jn 1:8).

Even Paul admitted this himself:

> *I do not understand my own actions. For I do not do what I want, but I do the very thing I hate. Now if I do what I do not want, I agree that the law is good. So then it is no longer I that do it, but sin which dwells within me.*
>
> *Romans 7:15-17*

SO WHAT ARE WE TO DO?

G od still, however, provides the way out, through the continuity of the atonement. There is much to say here, but
simply, "For our sake he made him to be sin who knew no sin,
so that in him we might become the righteousness of God" (2
Cor 5:21). The Apostle John also expressed this:

> My little children, I am writing this to you so that you may not
> sin; but if any one does sin, we have an advocate with the Father,
> Jesus Christ the righteous; and he is the expiation for our sins,
> and not for ours only but also for the sins of the whole world.
>
> *1 John 2:1-2*

For every individual faithful member of the New Covenant
Church, this involves:

- REPENTANCE (1 Jn 1:9),
- TURNING from sin and sinful
  passions (Rom 6:12; Col 3:5f;
  Eph 5:3-5);
- and, as Jesus instructed Nicodemus, looking to Jesus
  on the cross as our atoning
  SACRIFICE, for, as stated in Hebrews, "he has appeared
  once for all at the end of the age to put away sin by the
  sacrifice of himself" (Heb 9:26b).

ATONEMENT
Repentance
Turning
Sacrifice
Sacraments
Priests

■ We experience the graces of the atoning sacrifice of Christ through the SACRAMENTS of His Church. Most specifically and efficaciously, individual baptized members of the Body experience the power of Christ's atoning sacrifice through the celebration of the Lords' Supper or Eucharist.

■ Repentance, as in the Old Covenant, involves the intercession of the Apostles and their successors, the bishops and presbyters (or PRIESTS), which Jesus instituted through the ordination of His Apostles as the priests of the New Covenant:

Receive the Holy Spirit. If you forgive the sins of any, they are forgiven; if you retain the sins of any, they are retained.

John 20:21-23

HOPE?

Up through this point, there is amazing continuity between life as an individual member of the Old or the New Covenant families of God. Everything in the Old was touched, renewed, and fulfilled by Jesus; everything that was old is now new in Him.

In the context of hope, however, there are some **significant discontinuities** between the Old and the New, but these are explained through the fulfillment provided through the Incarnation, death, and resurrection of Jesus Christ.

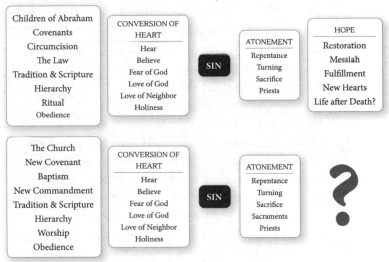

The most significant discontinuities are summarized by the author of Hebrews:

> *On the one hand, a former commandment is set aside because of its weakness and uselessness (for the law made nothing perfect); on the other hand, a better hope is introduced, through which we draw near to God.*
>
> *Hebrews 7:18-19*

The new aspects of this "better hope" deserve a more thorough exposition, but I'll just enumerate them:

- Members of the New Covenant Body of Christ have been CLEANSED FROM ORIGINAL SIN. As mentioned earlier, this doctrine of original sin was not fully recognized or defined in the early years of the Church, but the cleansing aspect of Baptism bringing new life was clear from the beginning (1 Cor 6:11; Col 2:11-12; 1 Pet 3:20-22; Rom 6:3-5). This wasn't possible in the Old Testament, but it is true now in Jesus through Baptism. We are able to stand before God with a clean slate, as new creations in Christ (2 Cor 5:17).

> Cleansed from
> Original Sin

- Members of the new covenantal Church receive the GRACE of Christ through Baptism and the other sacraments. It is this grace in fact that re-shapes most of the Old Testament categories into the new categories. As the result, being free from original sin and assisted by His grace, a person in Christ can resist "the world, the flesh, and the devil," obey the commandments, and a live holy life.

> Cleansed from
> Original Sin
> Grace

- As promised by Christ, children of the New Covenant Family of God have the HOLY SPIRIT, in fact the Trinity, dwelling within them. Though some in the Old

Testament had received the Holy Spirit, this indwelling of the Holy Spirit in the hearts of the baptized is an entirely new thing, promised by Jesus Christ (Jn 14-16).

> Cleansed from
> Original Sin
> Grace
> The Holy Spirit

■ As the Scriptures teach, one of the reasons that Jesus, the Son of God, became flesh was so that we might become PARTAKERS OF THE DIVINE NATURE. The Apostle Peter taught that this was the result of the many blessings we receive from Christ:

> Cleansed from
> Original Sin
> Grace
> The Holy Spirit
> Divinization

His divine power has granted to us all things that pertain to life and godliness, through the knowledge of him who called us to his own glory and excellence, by which he has granted to us his precious and very great promises, that through these you may escape from the corruption that is in the world because of passion, and become partakers of the divine nature.

2 Peter 1:3-4

■ As a result of all of the above, followers of Christ need no longer understand themselves as merely slaves to a master, creations to a Creator, sheep to a shepherd, but adopted CHILDREN OF GOD, "born, not of blood nor of the will of the flesh nor of the will of man, but of God" (Jn 1:13). And as Paul expounds:

> Cleansed from
> Original Sin
> Grace
> The Holy Spirit
> Divinization
> Children of God

...[A]nd if children, then heirs, heirs of God and fellow heirs with Christ, provided we suffer with him in order that we may also be glorified with him.

Romans 8:16-17

■ But therein lies a totally unexpected aspect of this new covenantal life: SUFFERING. Neither those in the Old Testament nor most contemporary Christians understand how to fit suffering into their theologies of an all-knowing, all-powerful, merciful yet righteous God. As declared above by Paul, however, we are children and heirs of God "provided we suffer."

> Cleansed from Original Sin
> Grace
> The Holy Spirit
> Divinization
> Children of God
> Suffering

As a Presbyterian minister, I had no categories in my theology for Paul's insistence on the necessity of accepting suffering, especially as he described it in his letter to the Colossian Christians:

Now I rejoice in my sufferings for your sake, and in my flesh I complete what is lacking in Christ's afflictions for the sake of his body, that is, the Church...

Colossians 1:24

But this was because I understood salvation basically as individualistic, rather than interconnected with other Christians in the Communion of Saints: the Church Militant (on earth), the Church Suffering (those who have died in grace and are being cleansed for entrance into heaven), and the Church Triumphant (the saints who have entered into the Beatific Vision). As Christ warned, particularly in His Sermon on the Mount, following Him involves sacrifice, sharing in His suffering, and as members of the Body, we share in each other's sufferings:

For the body does not consist of one member but of many ... If one member suffers, all suffer together; if one member is honored, all rejoice together.

1 Corinthians 12:14, 26

■ But the most significant difference between the Old and the New is the promise of ETERNAL LIFE and the resurrection of the body. Though those living during the Old Testament did not understand this, we now understand, through the revelation of God, that every individual person will live forever. The question is, where: either eternally separated from God in hell, or eternally with Him in Glory?

> Cleansed from
> Original Sin
>
> Grace
>
> The Holy Spirit
>
> Divinization
>
> Children of God
>
> Suffering
>
> Eternal Life

Many New Testament texts make this promise, but the following particularly makes this one discontinuous aspect of the New Covenant most plain:

So Jesus said to them, "Truly, truly, I say to you, ... he who eats my flesh and drinks my blood has eternal life, and I will raise him up at the last day. For my flesh is food indeed, and my blood is drink indeed. He who eats my flesh and drinks my blood abides in me, and I in him."

John 6:53-56

CONCLUSION

So, first: the following chart visually portrays the amazing continuity between the Old and New covenantal families of God. There is no "biblical interpretation of discontinuity" here, but rather a continuity of fulfillment in Christ of all aspects of life for individual members in the Family of God, the Church.

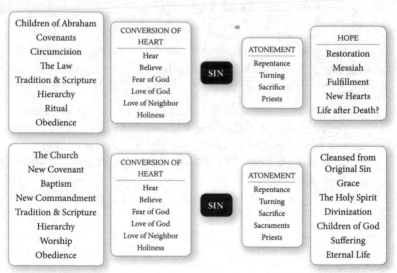

So, what about the Gospel message of John 3:16 or even the *Roman Road*? Within the full context of becoming, through Baptism, a member of the Family of God, the Church, these are true summaries of the Gospel. "Believing in Him" means accepting His whole Word, which includes the continuity of the Church ultimately as the means of salvation.

This continuity of the Early Church can be clearly seen throughout the writings of the Early Church Fathers. The following extensive quote, from *Against Heresies* by Saint Irenaeus, the Bishop of Lyon, was written around AD 190:

> *The Church, which has spread everywhere, even to the ends of the earth, received the faith from the apostles and their disciples. By faith, we believe in one God, the almighty Father who made heaven and earth and the sea and all that is in them. We believe in one Lord Jesus Christ, the Son of God, who became man for our salvation. And we believe in the Holy Spirit who through the prophets foretold God's plan: the coming of our beloved Lord Jesus Christ, his birth from the Virgin, his passion, his resurrection from the dead, his ascension into heaven, and his final coming from heaven in the glory of his Father, to recapitulate all things and to raise all men from the dead, so that, by the decree of his invisible Father, he may make a just judgement in all things and so that every knee should bow in heaven and on earth and under the earth to Jesus Christ our Lord and our God, our Savior and our King, and every tongue confess him.*

> *The Church, spread throughout the whole world, received this preaching and this faith and now preserves it carefully, dwelling as it were in one house. Having one soul and one heart, the Church holds this faith, preaches and teaches it consistently as though by a single voice. For though there are different languages, there is but one tradition.*

The faith and the tradition of the churches founded in Germany are no different from those founded among the Spanish and the Celts, in the East, in Egypt, in Libya and elsewhere in the Mediterranean world. Just as God's creature, the sun, is one and the same the world over, so also does the Church's preaching shine everywhere to enlighten all men who want to come to a knowledge of the truth.

Now of those who speak with authority in the churches, no preacher however forceful will utter anything different—for no one is above the Master—nor will a less forceful preacher diminish what has been handed down. Since our faith is everywhere the same, no one who can say more augments it, nor can anyone who says less diminish it.[1]

■ But Which Church?

But if this is true, what church today qualifies as this New Covenant Family of God—as the direct continuity with the Old Testament family of Abraham—the New Jerusalem?

If the Gospel is not about individualistic salvation—it isn't just "Jesus and me"—nor any random gathering of two or more believers in the name of Christ, then what about some local Presbyterian congregation? Or any individual local gath-

1   *Against Heresies* bk 1 chap 10 sec 1 (translation: *Liturgy of the Hours* ICEL 1974)

ering of Christians, regardless of denomination or tradition, especially one of those enormous independent megachurches, attracting thousands every Sunday and broadcast worldwide on television, radio, and the Internet? Do any of these demonstrate the continuity illustrated above, especially over a long period of time, for fifty, a hundred, a thousand years, or even "beginning from the baptism of John" (Acts 1:22), for if a church can't claim continuity from the beginning, in all aspects of what was presented above, then how does it fulfill the promises of Christ? (Mt 16:18; Jn 16:13).

I suppose different congregations or denominations have retained certain aspects, fragments, or permutations of this continuity. Still, isn't there one Church that still exists after two thousand years that has always claimed, accepted, and defended the responsibility and gift of this continuity, and still understands its mission—which the Lord entrusted to her to contend for the faith once for all delivered to the saints.

Even as I think of the answer, I'm hearing my own lingering prejudice cry out, "But what about the scandals and corruptions; the heretical and sinful men and women who sought after power and prestige, position and wealth in positions of that Church's leadership, rather than holiness, service, and love?"

In this, once again, we encounter continuity, for Jesus warned in His parable about the man who sowed good seed in his field, that, as this was a characteristic of the Old Covenant family of Israel, this would also be a characteristic of the New Covenant kingdom of God:

> So when the plants came up and bore grain, then the weeds appeared also. And the servants of the householder came and said to him, "Sir, did you not sow good seed in your field? How then has it weeds?" He said to them, "An enemy has done this." The servants said to him, "Then do you want us to go and gather

them?" But he said, "No; lest in gathering the weeds you root up the wheat along with them. Let both grow together until the harvest; and at harvest time I will tell the reapers, Gather the weeds first and bind them in bundles to be burned, but gather the wheat into my barn."

Matthew 13:24-30

And of course, this prophesied continuity immediately showed its ugly head within the hand-chosen Apostles themselves, with the betrayal by Judas, the denial by Simon Peter, and the cowardice of the rest. The failure of leaders in the Catholic Church does not disqualify her, but rather qualifies her to be considered as the one true candidate for this continuing New Covenant Family of God.

Some might also argue, "Well, what about the Eastern Orthodox Churches? They claim this direct continuity with the apostolic church?" I would simply answer that a quick glance into any phone book reveals the absence of unity so clearly apparent in the continuity between the Old and the New demonstrated above. The Orthodox Churches are divided churches, not one united Family of God.

■ One Last Thing

What about those who have never heard any of this? What about those who only have been taught an individualistic faith in Jesus *alone*? Or those who are blind to how individualistic their theologies are?

Again in this we see the continuity between the Old and the New. In the Old Covenant, if someone was outside of the children of Abraham and knew  nothing about the God of Abraham, Isaac, and Jacob, God would not judge them according to the ordinances of the law, but by the law that He had written upon their hearts:

All who have sinned without the law will also perish without the law, and all who have sinned under the law will be judged by the law. For it is not the hearers of the law who are righteous before God, but the doers of the law who will be justified. When Gentiles who have not the law do by nature what the law requires, they are a law to themselves, even though they do not have the law. They show that what the law requires is written on their hearts, while their conscience also bears witness and their conflicting thoughts accuse or perhaps excuse them on that day when, according to my gospel, God judges the secrets of men by Christ Jesus.

Romans 2:12-16

The same is true today for those, outside the Catholic Church, who do not *know* about the need to be a part of this one Body of Christ, the Church. The Catholic Church believes, however, that God will not hold individuals guilty for any lack of knowledge for which they are not responsible:

Those who, through no fault of their own, do not know the Gospel of Christ or his Church, but who nevertheless seek God with a sincere heart, and, moved by grace, try in their actions to do his will as they know it through the dictates of their conscience— those too may achieve eternal salvation.[2]

Catechism 847

The Catholic Church believes that this is also true for non-Catholic Christians: God will not hold them guilty for their ignorance, or the schisms that placed them outside the Church:

However, one cannot charge with the sin of the separation those who at present are born into these communities [that resulted from such separation] and in them are brought up in the faith of Christ, and the Catholic Church accepts them with respect and affection as brothers . . . . All who have been justified by faith in Baptism are incorporated into Christ; they therefore have a right

---

2 Quoting *Lumen Gentium*, 16.

> to be called Christians, and with good reason are accepted as
> brothers in the Lord by the children of the Catholic Church.[3]
>
> Catechism 818

This does not mean, however, that one can safely remain
outside the Catholic Church, relying solely upon one's personal relationship with Jesus, for the Catholic Church has always
taught that Christ intended there to be one united Church as
the one true channel of salvation. This is what Christ prayed
for in His great priestly prayer:

> *And for their sake I consecrate myself, that they also may be
> consecrated in truth. I do not pray for these only, but also for
> those who believe in me through their word, **that they may all be
> one**; even as thou, Father, art in me, and I in thee, that they also
> may be in us, so that the world may believe that thou hast sent
> me. The glory which thou hast given me I have given to them,
> **that they may be one even as we are one**, I in them and thou in
> me, **that they may become perfectly one**, so that the world may
> know that thou hast sent me and hast loved them even as thou
> hast loved me.*
>
> John 17:19-23

Therefore, though the Catholic Church is committed to
ecumenical dialogue and cooperation in love with other non-
Catholic Christians, yet she firmly teaches that if a person
knows that the Catholic Church is the continuing People of
God, the Church established by Jesus Christ in His Apostles,
then that person needs to respond in "obedience of faith"
(Rom 1:5), because, as has long been taught by the Church,

> [T]hey could not be saved who, knowing that the Catholic Church
> was founded as necessary by God through Christ, would refuse
> either to enter it or to remain in it.[4]
>
> Catechism 28

....

3   Quoting *Unitatis Redintegratio,* 3 § 1.
4   Quoting *Lumen Gentium,* 14.

As our Lord Jesus said, "Abide in me, and I in you ... for apart from me you can do nothing," (Jn 15:4-5) and the primary way a person is united with Jesus is through membership in His Body, the Church. This membership begins with Baptism, but, as Avery Cardinal Dulles, a prominent convert to the Catholic Church, explained, "Baptism is only the first sacrament of initiation and demands to be completed by the Eucharist."[5] Jesus Himself explained the importance of the Eucharist in the only verse where He specifically described how a person abides in Him:

> *He who eats my flesh and drinks my blood abides in me, and I in him.*
>
> *John 6:56*

Cardinal Dulles further explained:

> *The cultural atmosphere of our world inclines us to say that all churches and ecclesial communities, no matter what their tenets may be, are equally legitimate. The Church of Christ, according to this view, has been fragmented into a multitude of denominations, no one of which can claim to have the fullness of Christianity. Even Catholics frequently speak as though it makes no difference whether a person be Protestant, Catholic, or Orthodox. They sometimes speak as though a multiplicity of mutually complementary churches were the will of Christ himself.*

> *The Catholic Church has never accepted this outlook. It has insisted, and continues to insist, that the Church of Christ subsists in its fullness in the Roman Catholic communion and nowhere else.[6] The Catholic Church—and she alone—is equipped with the fullness of the means of salvation. All the blessings of the New Covenant have been entrusted to her alone, and whatever elements of the true Church survive in other communions derive from the Catholic fullness and belong by right to the Catholic*

---

5   "Vatican II and Evangelization," in Steven Boguslawski and Ralph Martin, Editors. *The New Evangelization: Overcoming the Obstacles* (Paulist Press: New York, 2008), 6.

6   Quoting *Lumen Gentium*, 8.

Church.[7] ... Until people have accepted the fullness of Christian revelation as proclaimed by the Catholic Church, their evangelization is not yet complete.

Another prominent former Presbyterian convert, Dr. Scott Hahn, confirms what has been summarized above in the following quotes:

The Church, therefore, is the renewed people of God, the "catholic" or universal family of God, opened to all so that they may embrace the God of Israel as their Father.[8]

The Church is the New Jerusalem. When we become members of the Church, we become citizens of the heavenly Jerusalem.[9]

Pope Benedict XVI has confirmed this when he wrote, "The early Church did not set herself against Israel; rather, she believed herself, in all simplicity, to be Israel's rightful continuation."[10]

The Protestant reformers were always quick to quote St. Augustine in defense of their theologies and resultant actions, but the following is one quote (among many) which they conveniently ignored:

A man cannot have salvation, except in the Catholic Church. Outside the Catholic Church he can have everything except salvation. He can have honor, he can have Sacraments, he can sing alleluia, he can answer amen, he can possess the gospel, he can have and preach faith in the name of the Father and of the Son and of the Holy Spirit; but never except in the Catholic Church will he be able to find salvation.[11]

---

7   Quoting *Unitatis Redintegratio,* 3.

8   Scott W. Hahn, *Covenant and Communion,* (Baker Brazos Press; Grand Rapids, 2009), 145.

9   Scott W. Hahn, *A Father Who keeps His Promises* (Servant Books: Cincinnati, 1998), 258.

10   Joseph Cardinal Ratzinger. *Pilgrim Fellowship of Faith: The Church as Communion,* 271; quoted in Scott W. Hahn, *Covenant and Communion,* 167.

11   *Discourse to the people of the Church at Caesarea,* AD 418.

In its context, St. Augustine was not speaking to those who had never heard about Christ or who were ignorant of the necessity of belonging to His Church, but rather to Catholics who were tempted to leave the Church, or who had left the Church and were in schism.

This being said, and in conjunction with all that has been discussed above, it would seem reasonable for anyone who desires to be saved—to do all that is within their power to attain eternal life, aided by grace of course—to consider the necessity of being a faithful individual in the New Covenant Family of God, the Body of Christ, the Catholic Church. To do otherwise is to take a precariously bold and individualistic stand in opposition to the consistent message of the Church, from Jesus Christ to His Apostles through the Early Church Fathers, on through all the popes, bishops, and saints of the past two thousand years, and consistently witnessed to and proclaimed by faithful Catholics today in every nation and culture.

Certainly there have been many within the Church who have failed to live faithfully what is expected and described above, but this is never an excuse for rejecting the Church established by Christ in His Apostles and gambling one's eternal destiny on individualism, or even gathering together with other likeminded individuals to form a "better" church based upon personal preferences or ideals. As Saint Paul warned:

> *For the time is coming when people will not endure sound teaching, but having itching ears they will accumulate for themselves teachers to suit their own likings, and will turn away from listening to the truth and wander into myths.*
>
> *2 Timothy 4:3-4*

This day has certainly come.

Are you certain that you can trust your eternity—your salvation—to the beliefs, doctrines, practices, and leadership presently guiding your life? Can you be certain that you can trust *yourself* to know and discern what is eternally true?

Jesus promised those who believed in Him,

> *If you continue in my word, you are truly my disciples, and you will know the truth, and the truth will make you free.*
>
> John 8:31-32

Can you be certain, as an individual seeking to follow Christ, that you are indeed *continuing* in His *word*? Is the Bible *alone* sufficient to do this, or does the existence of thousands of independent, contradicting, and sometimes combative Christian traditions and denominations prove that individual interpretation cannot be trusted?

If apart from Jesus Christ a person can do nothing (Jn 15:5), and if the witness of history has been that we are primarily united to Christ through the Church and her Sacraments, isn't it reasonable to beckon everyone to *come home* to the New Covenant Family of Abraham, the one, holy, Catholic, and apostolic Church?

FURTHER READING

Journeys Home, edited by Marcus Grodi; CHResources

Thoughts for the Journey Home, by Marcus Grodi; CHResources

How Firm a Foundation, by Marcus Grodi; CHResources

Pillar and Bulwark, by Marcus Grodi; CHResources

Christ in His Fullness, by Bruce Sullivan; CHResources

My Journey to the Land of More, Leona Choy; CHResources

Ignatius of Antioch and Polycarp of Smyrna: A New Translation and Theological Commentary, by Kenneth Howell, Ph.D.; CHResources

A Father Who Keeps His Promises, by Scott Hahn, Ph.D.; Servant Books

Born Fundamentalist, Born Again Catholic, by David B. Currie; Ignatius Press

Classic Converts, by Fr. Charles P. Connor; Ignatius Press

Crossing the Tiber, by Stephen K. Ray; Ignatius Press

Four Witnesses: The Early Church in Her Own Words, by Rod Bennett; Ignatius Press

Home at Last, edited by Rosalind Moss; Catholic Answers

My Life on the Rock, by Jeff Cavins; Ascension Press

One Shepherd, One Flock, by Oliver Barres; Catholic Answers

Rome Sweet Home, by Scott & Kimberly Hahn; Ignatius Press

Surprised by Truth, edited by Patrick Madrid; Basilica Press

The Eucharist for Beginners, by Kenneth Howell, Ph.D.;
  Catholic Answers

The Path to Rome, by Dwight Longenecker and Cyprian
  Blamires; Gracewing

There We Stood, Here We Stand, by Timothy Drake; 1st Books
  Library

AUTHOR'S BIOGRAPHY

Marcus Grodi received a B.S. in Polymer Science and Engineering from Case Institute of Technology. After working as a Plastics Engineer, he attended Gordon-Conwell Theological Seminary, where he received a master's in divinity degree. After ordination, he served first as a Congregationalist and then eight years as a Presbyterian pastor. He is now the President / Founder of the Coming Home Network International. He hosts a live television program called *The Journey Home* and a radio program called *Deep in Scripture,* both on EWTN. Marcus, his wife, Marilyn, and their family live on their small farm near Zanesville, Ohio.

For more information about the author and the Coming Home Network International, please write, phone, or visit their website:

The Coming Home Network International
PO Box 8290
Zanesville, OH 43702-8290
1-740-450-1175
http://www.chnetwork.org